IT'S A DAD'S LIFE

Edited By

TRUDI PURDY

First published in Great Britain in 1993 by
ARRIVAL PRESS
3 Wulfric Square, Bretton,
Peterborough, PE3 8RF

Foreword

Is that you on the front cover? Lazing in your favourite armchair, enjoying the peace and quiet, on a Sunday afternoon. The lawn has been mowed, the painting and decorating has been done and now it's time to relax. What better way to take time out than to read a book especially for you? *It's a Dad's Life* is here to say Thanks Dad! To give you that well deserved slap on the back.

The general feeling that you will get from reading the poetry included is one of light-hearted joviality. Some poems will definitely tickle your funny bone, some are serious and will make you think. The subjects, although based on Fathers, are varied, including poems about the birth of a child; the job that Dads do; missing Dad when he's gone; and even how one poet sees the first Fathers' Day happening on the Ark!

It's a Dad's Life is a book to treasure day in, day out. It will remind you of the person who gave it to you every time you pick it up. I know that you will enjoy reading *It's a Dad's life*: be it Monday, Wednesday or Thursday, pretend it is Sunday, sit back, and enjoy yourself!

Trudi Purdy

Contents

The Handsome Stranger

When I was three, Dad went away. To serve his country in the war.
And until I was eight years of age, of him I saw no more.
He served throughout the Middle East and did not come to harm
And returned, a handsome stranger, tanned by the desert warm.
He brought presents back for mother, and chocolate full of sand.
For me, a Fez, and a headdress, with a genuine Arab band.
He went to work, back in the shop. Where he had worked before.
There was rationing and shortages, resulting from the war
Yes life was hard in those days, things were very tight.
He cashed up and counted coupons, well into the night.
But we used to go on outings, having lots of fun.
On his BSA combination (when he could get the thing to run)
Now Dad is over eighty and still does a part time job.
When you're on the pension, you need the extra bob.
I have a sister and a brother. Another sadly died.
But Dad, I speak for all of us, we look on you with pride.

D Stevenson

Dad

I was always Daddy's girl and loved him very much,
Like my Mother he too had had, a very gentle touch.
When I sat upon his knee he'd gently stroke my hair,
I'd look up to him lovingly, so glad that I was there.
He always took great care of us, each and every one;
Doing many jobs each day 'till the hours were done.
Sisters, brothers, I had many, nine of us in all!
Big in heart and big in stature, over six feet tall.
He it was who took me fishing, taught me all the joys,
And of course along with me, his two youngest boys.
He was there all through my life to help and comfort me,
And we shared so many hours as happy as could be.
When fishing, just the two of us, we didn't need to speak
We shared a silence that was warm, (at least twice a week)
The year he died, for many months I shed a lot of tears;
But I was thankful that we'd shared so many happy years.

Doris J Baldwin

Dedicated to LAAA

My Father is a man
Who leaves each morning early.
Not exactly surly, but a proper business man.
Although he seems remote
He's doing all he can
This proper gentleman
To help improve the lot of his new tiny tot.

The passing years mellow.
this once remote fellow
Becomes more like a friend,
Sponsoring my education, aiding maturation,
Encouraging independence,
Yet swift with his assistance,
Even when I show resistance.

In time our new friendship
Takes on a third dimension.
As well as being my Father,
He's now a Grandad, rather
proudly holding each new grandchild.
He provides those extras which can't be afforded,
The number of cheques he writes, goes unrecorded.

But now he looks so fragile
In his gown so clean and white,
Lying in a hospital bed
He's still putting up a fight.
Our roles are now reversing,
And as I do the nursing.
It's me he will rely on to colour his horizon.

V Foggo

To You

To you who's
Fed me when I was hungry,
who's clothed me when I was bare.
who's loved, cared and nurtured me,
through times of bitter despair.

To you who's
Always there when I need you,
through the day and through the night.
who's hand is there to guide me,
to show me the wrong from right.

To you who's
Trusted in me completely,
even when I was unsure.
For giving me the reasons,
where no reason's stood before.

To you who's
Seen me grow from boy to man,
who's seen me selfish and kind.
Please accept this humble gift,
of these words I've tried to find.

I love you.

Steve Winter

Question for Dad

Why do trees and flowers grow?
Why does the sun give out a glow?
Why does the cold north wind blow?
Why is there such a thing as snow?

Why is there the runner bean?
Why is grass the colour green?
Why are ghosts so rarely seen?
Why must my hands be always clean?

Why is it that dogs have hair?
Why do the dead have eyes that stare?
Why sometimes are the trees so bare?
Why are two of things a pair?

Why is sleeping not much fun?
Why are there currants in a bun?
Why do bad men kill with a gun?
Why do they call me your little son?

Why is it that birds can fly?
Why are there clouds up in the sky?
Why do all old people die?
Why Dad . . . do you so often sigh?

Colin Needham

My Soldier Dad

'Your Father's home,' I heard Mum say,
As the key went in the door,
A scramble up the hallway,
Strong arms scooped me from the floor.
He'd been away a long, long time,
Away to fight the war,
Of course he'd done it by himself,
I was more than sure.
His army jacket felt so rough,
As I snuggled to his chest,
Fry's chocolate cream clutched in my hand,
My Dad, he was the best.
He was only home a day or two,
For then it was time to go,
When would he come home again,
We really did not know.
But sure enough the day did come,
When the dreadful war was finally done,
And once again I heard my Mum,
'Your Father's home, everyone.'

Rose A Coote

Thoughts En Famille

Patriarch I, at the table head,
Rebecca and Emma chattering -
Double delights for me instead
Of daughter never my own offspring.

Mother theirs, our Judith - gift,
Our caring, passionate dark-eyes;
Her liveliness our lives enriched,
Drawn to us by her marriage ties.

Eileen, my love, my dearest heart,
Your wifely presence bears on me
Two here live whole, two by part,
In our own conjoined ancestry.

Anthony sits next his mother -
Her elder-born, her first begot;
My outward self, yet much the surer -
Anthony, my calm, my confident rock.

Facing him is my younger son,
That inner me unrealized, desired;
My far-away Neil, my dreamy one
Contrived all that I once aspired.

Table-end opposite, Cathy's in place;
Cathy, our new daughter-to-be -
Catches my eye, lights up her face,
Glances a shy smile at me.

Cathy, I love our motley crew;
Cathy, your warm smile charms;
Cathy, I raise up my glass to you.
'Cathy! Welcome to our arms!'
W Roy Harvey

Thank You Dad

All those penniless
Nightshift years
Of hard work
Hard toil and tears
Summer holidays
Saved for carefully
And enjoyed so much

All those lectures
Wise words
And advice
Midnight curfew
Broken once
Never twice
For we feared you

All those talents
The knowledge
You possess
We watched
In awe
Always trying
To do our best

All those years
Carefree
Fun filled
Laughter years
Dad,
We love
And thank you for

Tina Gale

To Dad

It is a few years since you left us, still, our hearts are filled with pain,
Whatever life has in store for us, things will never be quite the same.

It is strange the things we take for granted, a look, a smile, a kiss,
We are ever discontented with things known as *Our Lot*,
Ever looking forward to what we have not got.

There is so much we should have said to you before you went away,
The pain and memories haunt us still,
Of your last living day.

It is all unfinished business and now there is not the chance,
We hope this dreadful experience, will our lives enhance,
It is all so very final and that is the hardest thing to bear,
We never realised how deeply we loved you, until you were not there.

You, though, in your wisdom, Dad,
And in your own very quiet way understood how much we loved you,
Before you went away.

We still love you very dearly,
And treasure the part in our lives you had,
To us you will always be a very special *Dad.*

Shirley Boyson

Domestic Disturbance

Father watched the twins at play,
During a school holiday,
Carelessly, around the well,
Into which, one screaming fell.
Father cried out, 'What a dunce,
Now I'm Father only once.'

Mother passing closely by,
Straightaway began to cry.
Saying, 'As I was his Mother,
We shall have to get another.'
Father called out in a fright,
'You know it is my billiards night.'

And as they spoke, the second twin
Searching for his mate, fell in.
Mother cried, 'That settles it,
I shall have to get some twit,
To do the necessary act,
With the maximum of tact.'

Father said, 'Now don't be daft,
We still have each other left,'
And consolingly enquired,
'Can't we wait till I'm retired,
At the age of sixty four,
And try for two or three or more?'

D T Baker

Oh Gentle Man

Oh gentle man so good and kind,
With generous thoughts in a gentle mind,
Who asked for nothing and gave so much,
A man of iron with a velvet touch.

Oh gentle man with a heart like a lion,
A tower of strength someone to rely on,
Courageous and honest, just and fair,
Loving and giving, eager to share.

Oh gentle man with knowing eyes,
And golden voice with words so wise,
Words that soothed like a gentle breeze,
Words to comfort, words to ease.

Oh gentle man how sad the day,
When we realised you could not stay,
For there's a place you have to go,
So sleep gentle man, you were an honour to know.

For Dennis Wall (1931-1992)

Julie E Wall

Jimmy Savile

If Jimmy Savile was my dad
I think I would be very glad
I could say 'Jim fixed it for me,
to go and live by the sea!'

We could run big marathons together
In the hot sun, or bad weather
On Sundays we'd sit by the telly
And on Mondays be sponsored to eat some jelly

'Dad, Dad,' I would say
'Can we open a supermarket today?'
'Now then, now then, my young son
I think we'd better ask your mum.'

When he goes for interviews
I'd clean his jewellery and brush his shoes
And as Jonathan Woss asks my dad
'How's your son? Good or bad?'
I hope he says, 'He's very clever
Never sad and couldn't be better!'

Because, then I'm sure I would be glad
If Jimmy Savile was *my* dad.

Kevin Winstanley

To My Daddy

Daddy, oh! Daddy, where are you now?
You left us when I was just four.
We wanted you always to stay with us,
Then you shouted and marched out the door.

Both of us cried for quite a long time,
We missed you so very much.
Mum said she'd be willing to take you back.
But you never did keep in touch.

I wish I could see you again one day.
Did you leave because I was bad?
Mum let me keep my picture of you,
Though she's torn up the ones that she had.

She goes to work now while I'm at school,
She says she has no other money.
I'm a big girl now - I'm nine years old -
I remember you called me your Honey.

I read very well and my writing is neat,
My arithmetic isn't so good.
I like drawing and painting, and playing at games,
And want to do French, if I could.

Mum has a boyfriend who loves us, he says,
And soon he'll be changing our name.
We'll have a new house, and I'll have a new dad,
But I'll still think of you, just the same.

Helena Kerr

Memories of my Dad

I've never asked for miracles
But today just one would do
To leave my door wide open
And see my Dad walk thro'
I'd throw my arms around him
And kiss his smiling face
For he was someone special
No one can replace
My heart is full of memories
With pride I speak his name
But nothing is the same
So Lord put Your hand upon my Dad
And give my dad some special care
Make up for all the suffering
And all that seemed unfair
Because my Dad and I
Had so little time to spare

Erimar MacMillan

The Bicycle

My Father knew that my son
Had grown out of his trike.
He answered an advertisement
For a second hand kids' bike.
He wheeled it home and hid it
In his old garden shed.
And worked out there every day,
Painting it gold and red.

He checked the tyres. Bought a bell.
Then polished it with pride.
Lovingly gave it to my son,
And took him for a ride.
My son pedalled joyfully,
To show his new prowess,
And I took my Father's arm and smiled
For he watched with tenderness.

Christine Pearce

Seventeen Long Years

Seventeen long years ago, I waved my kids goodbye
And as the train was pulling out, I began to cry,
I remember it like yesterday, on Glasgow Central Station
I thought that turning to the drink, would ease my situation,
I lost my home because of drink, and ended up in jail
I lay there lonely in my cell, my health began to fail
No once not twice but many times, I was in Barlinnie
A diabetic I became, just seven stone and skinny
Just three more years, you'll live my man, the doctor said to me
I thought, no I don't want to die, the pastor I will see,
The prison pastor, knew a place, he said I'll send you there
You'll be looked after, very well, by folk who really care,
So in a drunken haze I went, and settled in Dundee
And in that hostel I was loved, they took care of me,
Seventeen years have now passed by, and I am sober now
For with the help of God above, I beat the drink somehow
But I have never seen my kids, I'm really too ashamed
It's all my fault, and no one else, can possibly be blamed,
So when it comes to Fathers' Day, it matters not to me
For how can children send a card, to a dad they never see,
There's nothing I can offer them, for seventeen lost years
Except to say I was a drunk, I've cried a million tears,
I didn't set out, at the start, to be an alcoholic
I know now through my sober eyes, it was diabolic,
So to all fathers with their kids, I would like to say
Have a great time with your kids, when it is Fathers' Day.

David Wilson

When Father Was a Boy

In days gone by in Baldock town
When my Father was a boy
The pace of life was slower then
And people had little joy
Or did they, think awhile
Fewer houses then and shady walks a treat
Countryside for miles and miles
Life then was really sweet
As he remembers

School days, Gala days
Sticky sweets and Sexton Blake
All the world was at his feet
There was also Grandma's home made cake
A boy was always hungry
Pennies were very few
But if you could seek it out
There was always something he could chew
As he remembers

Football on a patch of grass
He who owned the ball had his say
Even though it was only a tennis ball
I must be Captain, or we don't play
Knickerbockers and Eton collar
Boots, the toes kicked in (from a photograph)
But such a saintly looking boy, I see
Well, it was all a good laugh
As he remembers

Robin Barker

Dear Dad

Children need much guidance
As they grow up and change
They need attention and love
To tackle the new and strange.

I can rely on you always
I know you're always here
To love and to help me
To shelter me from fear.

You mean so much to me
I appreciate all that you do
I am proud to be your child
And live my life with you.

Because you're very special
And always incredibly kind
I believe people like you
Are extremely hard to find.

So I'm sending you all my love
To you on Fathers' Day
Because I want to tell you
My love shall never stray.

Melanie Watling

Happiness to Gloom

Got married in seventy nine
To Anne who said she'd be mine
Evonne came along to make us three
That's the start of our family tree
Steven was born to make us four
Jan 1st, first footed our door!
Then my betting and drinking days
I seemed to get lost in a maze
Desperate times led to crime
I got thirteen year, in prison time
My wife had enough of this mess
Divorce granted, now they're one less!
That took them to a family of three
I killed the roots of our own tree
Now they've moved to another land
Anne now wears another's gold band
That's their family back to four
That hurts me, behind my door!
Can't see my kids, which is killing me
That makes in years, one, two, three
The kids only know their new Dad
That makes me feel so sad
Why am I so sad and blue?
Because I love them through and through
Look what I had, and what I lost
Lying in prison, counting the cost!

God bless both of you where-ever you are!
Love you. Miss you.
Your Dad.

Gordon Johnstone

Dad's Treasure

You make the twinkle in my eye
Gleam all so very bright
It's a pleasure to look after you
Such a treasured delight
Your curly little locks of hair
With eyes big and blue
I am so lucky to possess
A girl as beautiful as you
New things you learn from day to day
To crawl, to walk, to run
Seeing you each minute of time
It's truly so much fun
And perhaps in time, you never know
With luck with Mum and Dad
God willing we will have together
A lovely little lad.

Jan Nice

Proud Dad

I've witnessed the miracle of birth
in the early hours of the morn
on the 2nd July 1981 my son was born.

At 7lb 2ozs little Jon weighed in
a pink bundle of golden treasure
in monetary terms one cannot measure.

David Dawrant

Father Dear Father!

Dear Father we'll remember you
Every day our whole life through!
When troubles came what did we do?
It was to you your children flew!
No matter what, how deep the hurt,
Your sympathy was never curt!
Mother knew when you were there
She could leave us in your care!
Furthermore at weekends too,
The cooking could be left to you,
Year in, year out, the food you grew
Made sure we children never knew
What it was to be without a meal;
From the garden or orchard, where pigs did squeal,
Before they were ready to be turned into ham,
Spare ribs and bacon, a change from lamb!
Nor do we forget your devotion to mum,
Six decades and more together you'd hum
Those songs of old to our delight,
Then give us the works so we also might
Join in the singing, eyes shining bright,
And remember forever that enjoyable night!
Will I ever forget the times we spent,
You with hammer in hand, o'er the anvil bent,
A white hot plough coulter, for some farmer urgent,
We beat into shape, both with stern intent!
Not ever dear father, will we forget!
We children, who loved you, sincerely regret
That you did not make that century;
On which your heart was set!

Claude A Knight

Through the Eyes of a Child

My Daddy' s such a funny thing,
When he plays with me.
He'll give me a flip and a fling,
Then bounce me on his knee.
He'll throw me up into the air,
Then pretend he is a tree.
Yes Daddy's such a funny thing,
When he plays with me.

My Daddy's such a wise thing,
When he advises me.
He tells me to tie up my laces,
So I won't trip and skin my knee.
He says I've not to write on the wall,
And teaches me right from wrong and all,
And if I eat all my dinner, I'll grow big and tall.
Yes Daddy's such a wise thing,
When he advises me.

My Daddy's such a caring thing,
When he cares for me.
When I'm all tired he carries me up the stairs,
Tucks me up in bed, then helps me say my prayers.
Kisses me gently before saying goodnight.
Smiles at me warmly then turns out my light.
Yes Daddy's such a caring thing,
When he cares for me.

Yes my Daddy's just my Daddy,
He's better than fine gold.
There's nothing like your Daddy,
When you're a four year old.

Kevin Fitzgerald

My Dad!

An irascible man my Dad,
A man of *yan and yin*
Brilliant light and shadow
But oh I did love him.

Dedicated teacher, forceful head,
He loved the kids he taught.
Was strong and straight at all times
Respect to him they brought.

Blunt to the point of rudeness
But generous in his praise.
Found it hard to show affection
To us children that he raised.

A hearty laugh that bellowed out
A larger than life man!
Fastidious in his habits
Life with eagle eye he scanned.

Pipe always there, part of him.
Hair always short back and sides!
His frown could be a thunderous thing
But his smile was oh so wide.

His voice could be a bellow
But he was so soft within.
His good friends they all loved him
And how I do miss him.

Pat Rees

Downriver, Upriver

How strange that was! Steering downstream
to the city with my usual cargo,
  all the hard bargains I'd driven
  in towns of the interior, then
  seeing my son on the tow-path,
    heading upriver.

He was striding south towards the sun
which gilded his face and his matted hair.
  He smiled like one who heard
  his own deep music; tears
  ran glistening down his cheeks
    and shone in his beard.

That question to which we are the answer,
it's not up there, not where I've been.
  Big problems divide into smaller,
  which can mostly be solved, given time,
  but some interrogatives aren't
    real questions at all.

I wanted to hail him, even call out
some such words of advice, but we passed
  and the current pulled us apart.
  He hadn't seen, nor expected
  to find me there, an old trader
    quizzing his heart.

I watched his white-clad form recede,
then stoop to help some refugees
  from the endless civil wars.
  I was glad I'd not spoken. It's true,
  after all, that somewhere the river
    must have its source.

John Torrance

Daddies Girl

You've chubby cheeks and a button nose
Ten tiny fingers ten tiny toes
Big brown eyes and soft fair hair
Sleeping there without a care
You're talking now and walking too
I fetch you toys and play with you
A garden swing fixed in a tree
Sandpies and castles by the sea
On Monday now to school you go
Your pony tail bobs to and fro
As off to meet new friends you run
Laughing smiling having fun
A brand new bike you ride with ease
You joke with me and like to tease
Ballet shoes and dancing lessons
Jeans and shirts the latest fashions
On the telephone by the hour
Not a chance to get a shower
The little girl I loved so well
Has grown up now truth to tell
Boyfriends knocking at the door
Sporty cars exhausts that roar
Then the day that I've been dreading
Here it is your daughter's wedding
And as you walk her down the aisle
She turns and gives you one big smile
Later on with joy and laughter
You look again upon your daughter
A new life cradled in her arms
To tug your heart strings with her charms

M Burgess

Father and Son

Father, I want to be a doctor
diagnosing accurately
curing quickly.

Son, I promise you will.

Father, I want to be a professor
interpreting wisely
teaching clearly.

Son, I promise you will.

Father, I want to be a preacher
inspiring spiritually
living faithfully.

Son, I promise you will.

Father, I want to be a fisherman
trawling skilfully
landing successfully.

Son, I promise you will.

Father, I want to be a traveller
walking adventurously
living simply.

Son, I promise you will.

Father, I want to be a leader
managing effectively
earning loyalty.

Son, I promise you will.

Father, I want to live eternally
knowing our children
will always live hopefully.

Son, that all depends on you.

Heather Johnston

Thoughts on Fathers Day

Why do my thoughts flow thus, my passions inwards swell
Why this yearning in my heart, for why, I cannot tell.

Why do memories long since hidden, now appear before my eyes,
Why faint-hearted now I go, hold on to familiar ties.

Uncertainty and fears now lurk, within my beating breast,
And thoughts of age and greying locks, remind me of forgotten quests.

What in life have I achieved, what talents have I shown
What really in this uncertain life, can I feel to call my own.

The tragedies that Life has brought, the joys within my life
So balance, one with one against, happiness and strife.

So many things I should have done, still many yet to do,
And Time with every fleeting hour, my listless hands fall through.

Can it be I've lived in vain, what can my purpose be,
For why I feel so useless here, no future can I see.

For really I do know I'm loved, and love I've poured out too,
For bread upon the waters cast, what percentage will return to you.

How can I doubt within myself, how can I ponder here,
For love Divine, my soul doth claim, Drives out all earthly fear.

M Joan Winnington

Dad

Years ago when I was very small,
I didn't see much of my Dad at all,
He worked all day then went to the pub,
Only stopping off at home to eat his grub.

I remember most of all on a Saturday night,
He'd come home from the pub as high as a kite,
My mam was with him, her weekly treat,
Then off he'd go to a party down the street.

I remember sitting on my Dad's knee,
Sipping his beer, as happy as could be,
But come Sunday morning my Dad stayed in bed,
Moaning and groaning and holding his head.

When I see my Dad now we have a good laugh,
About long gone days and the old tin bath,
He only goes to pub now once a week,
Instead of a raver he's mild and meek.

Although a bit of a stranger when I was small,
I think the world of him and wouldn't swap him at all,
We've grown much closer over the years
So I'll raise my glass to him and say *cheers!*

A Ralston

A Cold Dawn

Last night I actually dreamt again,
I dreamt I walked the sweet shores of Paradise
And I wasn't alone Dad, you were there.
Univocal, the red roses of eternity
Rang to herald a Stoic peace
Rolling off the tongue, that was in keeping
With a kinder compassion, equal only
To that of existential mediation.
At first, morning brought with it a renewed
Anguish at your death, at my vulnerability,
Emotions rebelled, doubling their pathos.
Then, I stopped and for the first time since. . .
I smiled.

Gillian Luke

Dear Dad

When I grow up, I'd like to be
just like you, because, you see,
although I'm just a little lad
you are a very special Dad.
You urge me on to do my best,
not drift along with all the rest.
Improve myself in any way.
Put that bit more into every day.
One day perhaps I'll be a Dad.
A father to a little lad.
When that day comes, maybe I'll see
What it's like to have a pest like me!

Mavis Fox

I Should Have Listened to Dad

I couldn't wait
To close the gate
And leave the ancestral home
The grass wasn't greener
And folk were meaner
On the lonely road to nowhere
But I wanted to roam
How could I have known
On my own
Life held more than daydreams
More downs than ups
More ifs and buts
Or so it seemed
Now one thing's for sure
One bloke knew the score
I should have listened more
To *my Dad.*

Roy Whitfield

Memories Are Made of This

I remember spotting trains on Sunday
Though it didn't last that long
We'd sit and wait for what seemed like hours
And then two would come along
I remember fingers cold and blue
From sledging in the snow
And stopping every now and then
So the dog could have a go
I remember playing cards for pennies
After tuna fish for tea
I remember never-ending patience
And your selfless love for me
So now seems just the time to tell you
This is the bottom line
I love you Dad, for now and ever
And I'm so glad you're mine

Nikki Freestone

My Dad

My Dad was a toff, he really was,
one of the elite, simply because,
there wasn't anything that had him beat,
he could, out-think, outsmart, all other dads in the street.
Turn his hand to anything, yes he could,
lend a helping hand, always he would,
but he couldn't abide dishonesty,
and many's the time, he's walloped my brother and me,
we had told a white lie, and he found out,
boy, did his hand make us holler and shout?
Dad's only vice was the football pools,
we dared not speak, it was an unwritten rule,
with wireless turned up, and pencil poised,
he *even* shushed mum for making a noise!
the only time that he ever won,
was 3/6d, what a princely sum!
Still, what we lacked in money, was made up in love,
I'll always remember, my darling old man, my Dad the guv.

J Hawkins

I'm Visiting my Daddy by Kibby Whizzer

It's me again dear Daddy
Sending you this letter
To say when Nan told me the news
I couldn't have felt better.

It's almost here old Daddy
It's almost *The Great Day*
When Nan, and *Whiz* and Goodies
Will be on their way.

I lay here on my blanket
Pretending I don't care
Let someone try to stop me
On Sunday I'll be there.

I've got my lead and collar
I've got my dinner too
All ready for my visit
Dearest Dad, to you.

I could wag my tail off
But hard as I have tried
I only move my botty
Side to side to side.

I've had the promised *Baffy*
So I am smelling sweet
I won't disgrace you Daddy
On Sunday when we meet.

I hardly can believe it
I wonder, is it true
I'm half afraid to go to sleep
Case I miss out on you.

Nan has told me lots of times
I'm going on a train
Keeps on about the weather
And hoping it won't rain.

We shall brave the elements
No matter what it is
So, longing for next Sunday Dad
Love, and licks, from Whiz.
XX

Joyce G Tryhorn

My Dear Dad

You always meant the world to me,
A guiding star you could foresee,
You were so loyal - a dear kind friend,
Such care and goodness to the end.

I do recall the way you gazed
At your wee lass - her pranks appraised
And when some school-days seemed hard graft,
Dear Dad - 'twas you who always laughed:

You never failed to have the knack
Of finding way a joke to crack,
And even when life brought a trial,
A cheery word you could compile.

I cherished you throughout the years,
But there were times, I did shed tears,
'Twas not my wish to stay out late,
Altho' it was a teenage date.

I tried to give you hope anew
When time it came to comfort you
Together, we found joy to share,
Serenity was everywhere.

I watched you growing older, Dad,
Your waning smile made me so sad,
And faltering voice, a whisper now,
I kissed your lips and soothed your brow.

With dignity, you slipped away,
I'll ne'er forget that saddened day,
Past memories, ever, will caress
My future paths with happiness.
Joan Higgins

After Dad's Funeral

Driving carefully homebound after,
With June and Charles aboard,
Through the centre of mid-Wales
And parts of the National Park,
There were scenes I'd never seen before
Though I'd past through many times
The sky was far more bluer
And the green trees seemed to shine
The mountains, cleaner, came to me
Far nearer than er' before.

The Optician had said my eyes were weakening,
- Only due to age,
No cause for undue alarm,
They'll probably outlast your brain.

What it was that made things so
Is something I may never know.
Perhaps Dad's way
Of letting me know
All's well!
On the other side.

David Madeira-Cole

Dad's Day Dream

Mothers are one thing. Everyone knows
They like flowers and chocolates and beautiful clothes.
But Dad, ah! He's different, he's not keen on crocks,
Or slippers or hankies or three-quarter socks.

Now a bottle of whisky would go down a treat,
Or a ticket for *City* (with executive seat).
Or new set of golf clubs complete with a bag?
(There's as much chance of that as an XJS Jag!)

But when his day comes, in the middle of June,
Perhaps a CD with his favourite tune
Will be on the table, with cards from his kin,
And they'll know that he's pleased by his widening grin!

Peter Roebuck

Memoir

Edward aged fifteen, longed to travel, - the world was his aim.
Claimed he was eighteen, joined the Royal Navy, a Matelot became.
One day on leave, met Laura, and they liked each other,
She was only seventeen, but neither ever courted another.
In 1910, Captain Scott chose Edward for a polar trip,
To the Antarctic, in Terra Nova, a gallant little ship.

Tragedy struck in those temperatures well below zero,
And in 1913, the sad survivors came home, - each a hero.
That autumn, Edward wed Laura in a Hampshire priory town,
He joined London's Police Force, and there they settled down.
Two years later, my birth made him a proud, happy Pater,
And was delighted, when came a son, five years later.

Taught us wrong from right, many skills, - joined our games.
Helped, advised, encouraged interests, and our ambitious aims.
Took part in swimming, cycling, tug o' war, boxing and judo.
Gently tended injured creatures, - floored a villain with a blow.
Played several stringed instruments, liked banjo and mandolin best.
In bass voice sang various songs, and composed a march with zest.

At schools, clubs, social gatherings, lectured on his polar venture.
Was always very keen to inspire a spirit of adventure.
Built a working scale model of Terra Nova, ever to remain
His tribute to lost shipmates, and explorers of Antarctica's terrain.
For twenty-eight years a police officer, efficient, considerate and admired,
Served in foot, mounted and Thames divisions, before he retired.

Talked on Radio and Television, - could have been a famous name,
A respected, kindly, modest man, he sought no claim to fame.
The last survivor of that polar epic, in England still alive,
Was greatly missed, when in 1973, he died aged eighty-five.
His model ship, in a famous museum, displayed for all to see.
For my wonderful, beloved *Dad*, the finest memorial there could be.
Ethel L Thake

King of the Night

I walk proudly down the street
Holding my head high in the air,
Flicking my tail from side to side,
Stalking and staring without a care.

I go on the midnight prowl
Singing the songs of the night.
Warding off the opposition,
Malevolent and victorious in fight.

My offspring stretch far and wide,
Black, brown, brindled and white.
I am proud of my sons and daughters
All looking a marvellous sight.

My mates all parade in splendour.
Their owners wear a deep frown,
Because I have the best reputation
As, the smartest Tom cat in the town.

Emma-Jane Lee

I Could Read at Three

There were always books,
handled gently as
rare blooms picked in bud.
Inspirational dew
to a flowering intellect.
Knowledge seeds sowed
and nurtured at his knee;
the prize winning blossom?
I could read at three!

Father loved teaching,
whilst learning to grow
the rarest of hybrids.
From a mother devoted
to laughter and play,
father tired,
sweeping park leaves
on a bleak
Christmas Day.

His own glory
shrivelled, dulled,
like autumn's dead gold;
little brilliance there now
in a legend untold.
Forgotten and ancient,
never meant to be,
yet who really cares
that I could read at three?

L Turner

In Memory of Dad

A kiss for Daddy, I was taught to say.
To bridge the miles while he was away.
I still remember, though not even four.
His homecoming, at the end of the war.

Dad was two people, of one I was afraid.
He would bark out orders as if still on parade.
I can recall, that certain look.
I had done wrong, in my shoes I shook!

The other Dad meant a lot to me.
As often I would sit on his knee.
Stories of India, and Burma he would regale.
Egypt and France, tale after tale.

It was Dad who took me to the pictures.
On his Lambretta, to cricket fixtures.
We went chestnutting to Virginia Water.
Out and about, father and daughter.

He is no longer here, but in a better place.
The years without him have been hard to face.
In the scheme of things he played his part.
Dad, you remain forever in my heart.

Patricia Bannister

Solace at Solstice

Turn the light out, or close the door I pray,
It pains me to see him so and hurts to say
That he waits for new life, his old spent
Or fulfilled, or whate'er the intent
Of a young man with life untainted.
See, he sleeps. In soft thoughts unknown,
Seconds waxing, the solstice sun dies low,
Warming with a ephemeral glow,
He dreams what only fathers know,
In this magical time of day.

Now dappled with scheming shades of yearning dark,
A face, rick damask, where loving cares mark
A steadfast course along which pride is bought,
New life fashioned and solace sought
Here among the mazy hues.
Let the lights burn and close not this door,
Through which wonderful spells hold in awe
Those who watch and now see the truth,
That achievement and bliss need little of youth
Here in the very heart of kindred.

Simon Morgan

Memories

Dad, you never told us
That day you left for work
That you would not be home again
And that's what really hurt

We did not get a chance
To show how much we cared
To tell you that we loved you
And of the feelings that we shared

You were not there to share with mum
The advice that she gave to us
To help us make our choices
And to shape our life for us

It's over twenty years ago
Since that day you went away
But our thoughts are still of you
And of the memories that we shared

We know that it was not your choice
To leave us all so sudden
But God must have had a reason
To take you up to Heaven

I know one day we'll meet again
And our family will be as one
United in the love we share
In the house we have in Heaven.

Margaret Fleming

Guess Who

He loves you more than anyone,
He never lets you down,
He's a very special person
That you're glad to have around.

He never tires of playing,
He always makes you laugh,
He's ready to protect you
When Mum's on the war-path.

There's no problem that he can't sort out
No damage he can't mend,
And even if you're very bad
He'll always be your friend.

He's a brother and a cousin
And a nephew and a son,
He's an uncle and a husband
And a friend to everyone.

I'm sure you'd like to meet him
This man who's slightly mad,
Please step forward - take a bow,
Let me introduce, *my Dad.*

L Wall

To Dad - on Fathers Day

In person dear Dad you're not with me today
But Heaven is only a *Whisper Away.*
Always it seems, still by my side.
You share my days, to encourage and guide,
Just as you did throughout childhood years,
So full of laughter - so empty of tears.

Fathers' Day is special, feelings are expressed,
No use writing on a card, it could not be addressed.
Instead, I offer thanks for all the love we had.
I truly was the lucky one to have you for my dad.

Joyce Barker

My Special Dad

My Father was a special friend
His guidance helped me grow
He gave me everything he could
To him, much thanks I owe.

But no longer is he here with me
To a better place he's gone
I think about him often
And to his resting place I'm drawn.

I lay a flower upon his grave
Tell him all my doubts and fears
I listen to the gentle breeze
And soon I'm filled with cheer.

I leave - my heart is lifted
I feel confident - at peace
My mind, no longer troubled
I feel my love for him increase.

I know he's always guiding me
I feel his presence near
For all he did, I thank him
And I hold him ever dear.

Marjorie C Edgar

Dad's Little Girl

The knowledge of a Father's love
Is one of my life's many joys,
A magic bond that lasts through life
And nothing ever destroys.

Sweet memories of bygone times
The years when I was a kid,
When I was always *helping* Dad
With everything he did.

Digging the garden or painting a wall
I remember the fun that we had,
Photographs taken down by the sea
Were always of me and my Dad.

When ever I've needed a chauffeur
If the weather's been sunny or bad,
I've known straight away there's no problem
I can always rely on my Dad.

Then came the day when I married
To give me away made him sad,
But he needn't have worried about losing me
'Cos I'll always be here for my Dad.

People still say that Dad spoils me
By giving in to each fad,
But I know it's done 'cos he loves me
And I *sure as hell* love my Dad.

Now Dad's retired we sit and reflect
On the years that have passed in a whirl,
And we smile at the memories and know in our hearts
I'll always be Dad's little girl.
Carol Francis

Time Sonnet
(For my Father)

If I could wipe away the lines
that tears and age, born of time
have etched upon Your loving face.

If I were conqueror of age
to turn back clocks, this helpless rage
that watches years roll one on one.

If I could see You young again,
free from time's relentless pain
free from clouds, stalking death,
free to love this world, but yet

You tell Me that You would not change
a single year, nor yet a day

with love of life, a fragile flower
I will love You, as You are.

J N Cates

Daddy! Please Come Home

We were shopping, Mum and I,
When I saw Dad go driving by.
He didn't see us - not aware
That Mum and I were standing there.
I called out, but he didn't hear -
Didn't know that we were near.

Late that night I couldn't sleep -
The pain in me beyond belief;
I asked of Him who is in Heaven
To listen to a girl of seven,
And make my Mum and Dad once more
As loving as they were before.

Every night I prayed in vain
My Daddy would come home again.
I hoped that when I woke one day
He'd be there to say he'd come to stay -
That he and Mum had kissed and we
Were going to live so happily.

Daddy! Don't leave us on our own,
Please Daddy, please come home.

John Castel-Nuovo

My Dad

My Dad he is the very best
In all the world it's true,
And of the nice things that he does
I'll tell you just a few.

He always mends my broken toys
And helps me with my sums,
Sticks-up for me if I *feel sick*
When School on Monday comes!

Together we have lots of fun
When he comes home at night,
And later, when Mum's back is turned
We have a pillow fight!

He's very caring is my Dad -
He gives me many treats,
And when I have been very good -
Buys me my favourite sweets.

Though he gets cross if I am rude
To Mum, or play a prank,
He chases me and when I'm caught
Gives me a botty spank!

The bully-boys who hang around
To try to frighten me,
Take one look at my big Dad
And suddenly they flee!

It's always great when he's around -
With him I'm never sad,
I'm really happy that dear Mum
Chose him to be my Dad.

Briony V Lill

The New Father

I'm going to be a Father, Dad, tell me what to do.
I want to teach my son, Dad, the things I've learnt from you.
I can't tell you it's easy Son, that would be a lie,
When you're woken up at midnight by your baby's cry,

It can be taxing on your nerves, of that there is no doubt,
All those feeds and nappy change, you'll have your work cut out.
But when he utters his first word, he'll make you feel so proud.
It's a very special moment when he says *Dada* out loud.

And when he gets all active, and is anxious to explore,
He'll rope you in to hide and seek and crawling round the floor.
Together you'll have so much fun, playing football on the beach,
Flying kites, and catching crabs. (Things his Mum can't teach).

And when the day comes to go to school, as you know it is a must,
You'll help him with his homework, in you he'll place his trust.
And when he is of age and asks about a girl,
Teach him the art of courting, his life will be a whirl.

Don't let him grow up too quickly, Son, let him take his time,
And then one day he'll come to you with all this on his mind:
I'm going to be a Father, Dad, you'll know just what to say.
You won't have to think about it, Son. Remember us today.

Sharon L Forsdyke

Father Figure

A Father Figure,
What is that,
A funny fellow in a hat,
Knobbly knees,
Fading hair,
Someone sitting in a chair,
Does it matter who he be,
As long as the model,
Is made perfectly.

Pauline J Crossland

Stigma

they gave you a dose of electric shocks
and locked your door
it's too far to visit
my mother said
Never mention

home for weekends
with hand woven footstools
you tried to make friends with my mother
she cringed
Never mention

Box Hill in the heat
I was sixteen
you convalescing
sat on the grass and watched me
revising

I saw you'd been ill
not *pretending*
outdoors
enjoying
I wanted to mention

indoors
destroying
he's seeking attention
shuttered affection
Never mention

Daphne Harrall

Remembering Dad

Dear Dad, I remember your letters coming
When we were far apart
Always very jolly and words straight from the heart
You liked to have your bit of fun
And to make the joke complete
You always added ha-ha, ha-ha
Keep your chin up till we meet
Another thing you always wrote
Was, to my little Jenny Wren
Which wasn't really my name of course
But only my state just then
Always up to all the tricks
You said, 'Show your officer this letter
And you'll get compassionate leave
Until your mother's better.'
When I was home on that leave
Your funny songs you sang
As all about the house you went
Your operettas rang
Putting your own words to well-known songs
And you did them justice too
No wonder you were happy then
You'd waved the army toodle-oo
Later opening a joke shop after heart-attacks
Your humour never failed you
Somewhere you and others laughed
Suffering a serious illness some many years after
At the funeral we all said,
You'd appreciate the laughter.

Connie Moseley

Fathers Day Poem

The day for remembering fathers is coming near,
But for you Dad shall I shed a tear?
Or sit and wonder, what it would have been like
To have you close and hold me tight.

Before my second birthday had come,
You decided to up and run.
Leaving behind a trail of mess,
To take your place in the world of rest.

Is it nice up there in the sky,
Watching angels flying by?
Laughing at the world below,
Trying to give their lives a go.

And were you really sorry to depart
From this life to the one above?
And can you really say you'd rather be
Here on earth, alongside me?

I wish you'd loved me enough to stay,
And follow me through to this very day;
Onlooking as I received my rewards
Proud to have this daughter of yours.

But if you think I hate you,
You are mistaken
I love you Dad, though you are in Heaven.

Helen Jackson (15)

Now I Understand

Now I understand why,
But at the time I resented your questioning,
And insistence on early homecoming.
I grew angry, rebellious,
And forgot the happy early years
Of companionship and trust.
Outings to sea and country
Surprises, presents, treats.
I could not, would not see
That your concern was for my welfare.
But now I understand -
Having children of my own
I share your anxiety.
I wish I had understood then.

I E Allpress

My Father's Thumb

It was there for me when I was small,
me being short, he being tall.
He walked with his hands behind his back
and I would follow in his track.

His glove button would be undone
and the lining fur would show, dark brown.
I couldn't hope to reach his arm,
so I held his thumb to keep me from harm.

When we crossed the street, his hand would slide
down to my level at his side.
But once over, back we'd be,
his hands clasped behind, with his thumb for me.

I held that thumb through several years,
Although I grew to reach his ears.
Then times changed, as they do,
now, I have my family too.

But when I visit my Dad again,
and we wander the streets, it's just the same,
he clasps his hands, as he's always done,
and I hang onto that comforting thumb.

Dorinda Smith

A Time to Laugh

Sadly, I lost my Father many years ago
But the memories I hold have never died
He had a wonderful sense of humour, a clever wit
He made me laugh at times when I could have cried

When I was feeling sad or down at heart
He'd say something funny to make me smile
He'd tell me a joke to cheer me up
He made me feel better in his inimitable style

There's a lot of sadness in the world today
And we all have our troubles, it's true
But we should try and be cheerful for my Dad taught me
When you laugh the whole world laughs with you

C R Maggs

It Was You

Who was there when I was wee
Who was there when I cut my knee
Who tied it up with a hanky so white
Who was there when I said night night

Who laughed when I had tugs in my hair
It was alright for you - your head was bare
Who taught me to ride a bike
Who did I trail after when he went for a hike

Who made my sledge when the fields were white
Or knocked down the chestnuts with all his might
Who let us chase rabbits in the harvest field
Who put up the stooks to make us a bield

Who came to meet me after the dance
Who stood at the door - escape - there was not a chance
Who gave up his time to see all was right
Who gave me his love morning noon and night

Why Dad it was you that did this for me
I didn't always like it didn't you see
My friends would laugh when they saw you there
But I knew you loved me and you showed you did care.

Nancy Scobbie

Dear Dad

Father's weather beaten face
A story in every line
Sailing on the seas of life
Through stormy winds of time
Bringing back from troubled lands
All things we need to know
And with a gentle smiling face
Watching over us as we go
Through a life of hills and vales
So happy and so sad
Holding on to a dream
Of a dear and loving Dad.

John William Bowen

Daddy Mine

Daddy dearest,
Daddy mine,
I miss your guiding hand
Your loving embrace.
It seems so long
Since I heard your voice
Or felt your love.
The loss has been so great,
Almost too great to bare.
No more the words of wisdom;
No more the looks we'd share.
Alone in my room
My heart is heavy
My eyes fill with tears
Daddy dearest, Daddy mine.
Will the ache of your passing
Ease with the passing of time.
I shall never forget
That special something you gave
That beautiful warmth
From a generous heart.
I will always remember
Even thought we're apart.

Josephine Blyth

Fathers Day Thoughts

Around comes Fathers' Day,
Once again;
Yet it brings no happiness,
Just continuous pain.
It's the first Fathers' Day
That without you will pass.
It's torture is evident
And for years it will last.
Just five and a half months
Since you passed away,
And changing seasons
Bring round Fathers' Day.
I remember past times,
The happiness gone by,
But they don't make me smile;
They force me to cry.
Oh Dad, I miss you.
I want you back;
The world is a cage
And my future seems black.
Around my young life,
There is a wall,
And coping with Fathers' Day
Is the worst part of all.

Gianna Pollero (14)

Who's Dad

These men, with creeping, grasping, middle age,
They're the men who wrote history's greatest page,
That man with greying, balding head,
Was he one who saw a nation's dead?

The fields of Normandy again,
Were strewn with wounded, dying, slain,
The filth of Burma's jungles steam,
Buried others of this nightmare dream,
Prison camps, seas cold and high,
Claimed the others who had to die,
Yet some came home, to mention the story,
Of heroes who died for little but glory,
But don't let us forget what these men have done,
When prayers are said for those who have gone,
They to gave of their best, they gave all they had,
Is it one of these men whom you call Dad?

M S Luke

What About me, Dad?

We always talk
About the weather
The boys, the neighbours,
The world in general.
What you have done
This week, no different
From last.

We *never* talk
About me. We can't.
We have left it too long.
Anything I do or say
Is beyond your understanding
Of the child
You cradle in your mind.

Margaret Williams

Father?

Definition; One who gives life, one who cares,
One, who when you need him is always there?

Someone who runs to pick you up when you fall and hurt your knee,
Who clambers up to rescue you when you're stuck up in a tree,
Who works so many hours to be sure you're clothed and fed,
And is always there to say *goodnight* when you are tucked up in your bed,
One who sits up worrying when the hour is getting late,
Yet disappears so quietly when he hears the old latch gate,
Who willingly would give to you his last half-penny piece
And mends the puncture in your tyre though he's tired and wants to sleep.
This person is not Father as the dictionary would describe,
But you could get no closer no matter how you tried,
This man who means so much and gives far more than I can say,
My stepfather, more Father in each and every way.

Gwen Collins

Reflection

I feel a . . . something
In my mind
It's presence is disturbing.
It seems to say
You've lost your way
I find it most perturbing.

Why aren't you free?
It says to me
This lurking thing within
And life is painted all in grey
For things that might have been.

Why bother me?
Please let me be
My course is now well set.
I have achieved so many things
And yet. . . (it seems to say)
And yet. . .

There was a time of aspiration
A zest for life and
Dedication to bringing others joy.
What became of me?
Where went the boy?

Alfred Dewsbury

Fathers

Fathers come in many shapes and size,
Different coloured skin and hair and eyes,
Though they differ you'll agree,
They all have expertise
In caring for their little girls and guys.

Fathers can create a lot of fun,
Giving piggy backs, and playing tick and run,
And on holiday it's grand; they make castles in the sand,
For their children, by the seaside, in the sun.

Fathers can make everything alright,
When you hurt yourself, or when you feel uptight.
And they gently stroke your head, as they tuck you up in bed,
Making all your dreams so happy, sweet and bright.

Ruby Anderson

Dear Dad

A war came between us when I was a child,
And we were far apart.
But you wrote to me from far and wide,
To show I was still in your heart.

In my teens, you taught me how to fight
For honour, for need, and for my right.
You showed me how to live my life
To standards high, and not to lie.
To work and play, and make you proud
Of me. . . not see me cowed.

You gave me away on my wedding day,
But remained by my side as a friend.
My ally in all things, when needed;
A shoulder to cry on. . . no end
To the things you would do for me,
My Father, so strong and so true.

I owe to you the person I am.
Dearest Dad, I'll always love you.

Carole Wills

One September

You never said.
You never told me you were going away
I never dreamt
I love you so
Why didn't you let me know
You were strong
They never said
How long must this torment last
You went so fast
I never said goodbye
Things were never said before you died
I saw you lying there,
So beautiful, so strong
I wanted to be wrong.
Oh Dad I miss you so.

Margaret Fitchett

To the Memory, Ever Dear

I only had him for a short time
but he managed to impart
all the knowledge and the know how
to give me a good start.

He taught me what was important
and to always do my best
to see the good in people
never mind the rest.

He always gave me lots of love
but plenty of discipline too
had the time to listen
and see my point of view.

I was only ten when he was lost at sea
but my memories of him never dim
he was all a good father should be -
and I thought the world of him.

Dorothy Baines

Dad I'm Sorry

Hello Dad, remember me,
long time no see.
My fault really, should have kept in touch.
Never thought I'd miss you so much.

Sorry Dad, I meant to write.
I never will forget that night.
A stupid argument which turned to a row,
and all the horrid things I said seem so silly now.

Dad, there's this girl I've met.
You'll like her I know, a real pet.
I'd like to bring her over for you to see,
I know she's the only girl for me.

Alright Dad, if that's how you feel,
it doesn't matter, no big deal.
I'd hoped we might be friends again,
didn't realise I'd caused so much pain.

Bye Dad, see you sometime.
If you change your mind just drop me a line.
I've said I'm sorry, I meant it too.
If I can forgive, why can't you.

David T Wicking

Dad

You were a Dad I was proud of,
You were a wonderful friend,
I loved you so much, my dearest,
And I did right up to the end,
When the doors of Heaven opened,
I knew you'd walk, right through,
And God would be there to reward you,
For all the things you did do,
When I was hurting, you held me,
And when I needed advice,
You would show me the way, Dad,
In a way that was truthful, but nice,
If ever I needed some pennies,
Your pocket, you'd dig, very deep,
And giving me all you had, there,
You'd do it, with never a peep,
So much you gave of yourself, dear,
With never a selfish thought,
Love and caring and giving,
Are gifts, that cannot, be bought,
So Dad, I say a big, Thank You,
And Heaven can't keep us apart,
For in thoughts, we're always together,
Linked by our Love and our Heart.
Your everloving daughter,
Janette.

Janette Campbell

Shadows

Old man sitting, head bent low,
Are you only aware
Of a life serene and the years between
As you smile and blankly stare
And muse on secrets that you alone know?
Misty shadows flit around,
Your confused mind, searching till you find
Some familiar sound,
Or well-trod ground
Where once you stood. Although
Shadows haunt and still abound,
Yet silently you sit, head bent low.

Once there was no time to pause
You stood erect, with head held high
Pursuing your goal, as life took its toll,
Yet no desire to rest or sigh.
Ambition ruled, no time to pause,
Years stretched ahead like a vast plan,
New roads to travel, themes to unravel,
As boy changed into man.
Once you thought for me, Dad, and because
I remember clearly, I can
Think for you, now, while you pause.

Sheila McGuire

The Worlds Greatest Father

Have you noticed that childlike faith,
of a little boy toward his wonderful Dad.
It holds something we can never replace
The wonder and joy of that little boy,
is written all over his face.

He'd rather have Father than silver and gold.
The story within him too much to unfold.
Will he? One day grow up the same way
Perhaps we will never be told,
until that little boy also grows old.

We all have Father in Heaven above
Whom, our eyes cannot see His love
but, somehow we know that He is
listening to you and to me,
and will answer our call whatever our plea.

Stan Gates

My Hero

My Daddy is a hero,
I'm proud to say,
fighting for our freedom,
showing us the way.
He said that he will think of me,
every single day,
and I've got to be the bestest girl,
while he is away.
So handsome in his uniform,
tall and brave and smart,
he said he'll keep my photograph,
right next to his heart,
and when the war is over,
we're going to do so much,
he said we'll travel everywhere,
it will all be such a rush.
He promised me I'd be his darling,
always and forever,
'till the day I marry,
we would always be together.
But Mommy told me, just today
that Daddy's not coming back,
he was killed, a hero, on the field,
in an enemy attack.

My Father died a hero,
I should be proud they say,
I'd rather him be nobody,
and to have him here today . . .

Belinda Freeman

My Dad

Dad you are so special to me
You're kind tender and true
When I think of all the love that you give
I'm proud to be part of you.

You taught me to respect people
No matter what colour or creed
And never mix with so called friends
Who's minds are filled with greed.

You took me to the seaside
When I was just a lad
We had so many wonderful times
You always made me glad.

You told me to help others
Who are not so lucky as me
Like children without fathers
That have never seen the sea.

I will always love you Father
And cherish the moments we had
I have many happy memories
Because you're my special Dad.

Hugh Amott

In Memory of my Father

Tho' years have gone
And memory is dim
Yet I still do
Remember him
My Father.

He took us to school
And fetched us back home.
He'd not allow
Us to go alone
My Father.

He worked at night
Was home in the day
And spent much time
With us in play
My Father.

When bombs crashed near
To our front door
And we all fell
Upon the floor
Our childlike hearts
Never knew fear
Because of
Our Father.

If he were now here
On Fathers' Day
I would make him
A great display
His love to us -
I would repay
Our Father.
Jeanne Boffey

Dad

So silent is his mourning
So great his deep despair.
Will we ever reach him?
Lord take him in your care.

You know his thoughts are lonely
His blackness deep throughout.
You now his heart, his mind, his soul,
Please, Lord seek him out.

He's so precious and so dear to me,
His pain I cannot bear.
Help him Lord I beg you. . . get him out.

He's so wonderful a Father
So strong, so straight, so fair,
A girl could want no other
To guide her along the way.

Lord don't ever leave him,
Although he has no faith

He'll come one day, I know it,
He needs your tender care.

Lord keep him close beside you,
Be patient, loving and wise.

That man is your child, you know it,
That's why he'll never die.

Some day he'll see the sun rise
He'll smile again, you'll see.

My Dad, my living hero,
So precious, so dear to me.

C Symm

Father

Dad's the one who wears the trousers *I think*
And does all the dirty jobs *perhaps,*
He's definitely the one at the kitchen sink
After a Sunday drink with the chaps.

Dad will cook when mum's not in
So you can all sup,
You can eat it or put it in the bin
At least it will fill you up.

He can't help it if he's not mum
At least he'll always try,
He'll look after you in his way
Basically he's a good guy.

He's been called dad, father and pop
But it does not matter really,
He doesn't care which one he's called
For he loves you all very dearly.

Alfred Saunders

Father

Father you're so very good
All my troubles understood
When my thoughts are not too clear
I know you have a listening ear

Memories of times in the sand
Of walking along hand in hand
Stories that are in my head
The ones you told me in my bed

Your advice I didn't always take
But you gave me room when I made a mistake
I used to pray and thank God above
For a Father who made clear his love.

Not by cuddles and stroking hair
But by letting me know he was always there
If times were good or times were bad
For having you as a Father I was always glad

As I mature and you go grey
Perhaps I'll get a chance to repay
You for all you've done for me
You're a figure of serenity.

Jennifer Ann Reid

To my Papa

My Papa always had a joke,
He never drank,
He didn't smoke.

An honest man,
You bet your life,
He lived for children,
Home and wife.

Papa never would complain,
Though he'd be out working
In sleet and rain.

He made dark days seem so bright,
He wheeled and dealed,
Both day and night.

He carried loads
Upon his back,
You'd think his bones
Would surely crack.

There's so much more
That I can say,
About love he gave us,
Day by day.

Of his strength and courage,
I could shout out loud,
But I'll simply say,
Of Papa, I'm mighty proud.

Cathie Wayne

My Father

I threw a net of words high into the air,
And tried with all my might to capture a star,
I pulled and pulled but soon got bogged down,
Yet I am glad the star is still there.

It's the same when I try to recapture Dad:
Brown-eyed, raven haired, singing, yes, always singing,
Patient, diligent, sober man of God,
Laughing, he'd set all hearts a-ringing.

Swimmer. Lover of nature, athlete,
Soft-hearted, gentle as a lamb.

All these words give some idea of Dad,
But a portrait needs a better artist than I am.

Mary Frances Mooney

Regrets

He has always been there
To help me through each day,
If I was uncertain
He would show the way.

When I was sad he cheered me
Never let me down,
However he was feeling
I never saw him frown.

He worked so hard to clothe me
Made sure I was fed,
I knew how much he loved me
From what he did and said.

I could never tell him
Just how much I cared,
I wanted to so often
But my soul would not be bared.

I thought there would be time
To tell him how I felt,
Neither of us prepared
For the card that fate had dealt.

Now it is too late
So little time he had,
And he devoted it to me
I'm glad he was my Dad.

But now I regret so many things
I wish I could have said,
How much he really meant to me
Too late, now he's dead.

I think he understood me
I feel without a doubt,
Because love and understanding
Is what life is all about.

Shelley Thomas

To Dad

I've always meant to tell you,
Yet could never find the words.
But I hope you know I love you,
My saying the words you've never heard.
We've had our ups and downs Dad
Yet, lately I've come to know.
That when my life gets really bad
You're on my side and love me, so
Here in verse are these few lines,
Telling you I really care.
We've had such a lot of good times,
I hope we've many more to share.

Hazel Jackson

Fathers Day

Why Dad should I acknowledge you?
I have not fond memories of the past,
like some.

I cannot remember sitting on your knee,
reading, talking, laughing, you
tickling me.

I cannot remember as a child
When fear took hold of me, at night.
You saying 'Come son, to my bed,
I will comfort you.'

If I did good, you did not praise
If I did wrong, you did not chastise
I was just there, to be ignored.

I'll just ignore Fathers' Day
In the same way as he ignores my birth.

Brian Walker

My Father's Son

Large callused hands held him aloft,
With eyes of ice yet strangely soft,
To welcome as *the day was done,*
The arrival of his only son.

'What kind of future will these eyes see?'
The father asked as he cradled me.
He sighed aloud as the memory stirred,
That awful day the townsmen heard
'The factory's closing,' the young man said,
'Give us this day our daily bread.'
The town fell silent and duly prayed
and dark shadows queued for benefit paid.

A man walked on with hope by his side,
Seeking out work still keeping his pride.
In another town he found his way,
'Working again, God bless this day!'
My mother cried as she hugged the man,
Who had done everything a husband can,
To ensure his ever faithful wife,
Would never to go without in life.

I am my Father's only son
and I wonder too how my life will run.
I cannot change the powers that be,
But will strive to be as proud as he.

Hazel Webber

Enniskillen

Father, hold my hand,
In darkness falling
Hold my hand,
Father, hold my hand,
Hear my voice calling,
Hold my hand.

For now the light is fading,
The dust is gathering,
The earth is cold,
For now the time is wending
And day is ending,
The hour is old.

Mari, hold my hand,
In darkness falling
Hold my hand,
Mari, hold my hand,
I hear you calling,
Hold my hand.

For now the light is failing,
The shadows creeping,
The earth is stone,
For now the time is sighing
And day is dying,
The hour is gone.

Father, I hold your hand,
In my going
I hold your hand -
Mari, I hold your hand,
Love everlasting,
I hold your hand -
Esme Francis

To my Dad

A happy childhood I know I had
with you in charge my dearest Dad
You taught me how to play some games
and told me all the fancy names
of flowers blooming in the park
and stars that glowed bright in the dark
I know I gave you lots of pain
when my own way I didn't gain
when in your heart you felt regret
as I got into a real real *pet*
Too late now to say I'm sorry
and to take away the worry
But as you gaze down from above
you'll know I've always felt your love.

Isobel Clanfield

Our Dad

When our Dad retired from the foundry,
we gave him a hearty big cheer.
He'd had no golden handshake or timepiece,
just a gurgling belly of beer.

To lower the cost of the food bill,
he'd shop on the cheap side of town,
but his shoe leather wore out quite quickly,
and the bus fare would cost half a crown.

Soon bored, took a job with the council,
in summer he sported a tan.
The kids held his hand very fondly,
their favourite *lollipop* man.

Then painting became an obsession,
not landscapes or portraits so sweet,
tin baths, brass door knobs, the bird cage,
'till mum yelled, 'I'm stuck t'loo seat!'

Our dad told us he wasn't lucky,
but I wasn't convinced of that.
On his bald head one summer in Blackpool,
a very brave seagull went *splat!*

Sadly he is no longer with us,
when my time's up, again we will meet.
A throne he'll be busily painting
- jade-green, to match the loo seat.

Wendy Morris

Pure Love

I sometimes wish that I wasn't a Father
It's not all it's cracked up to be,
Changing a dirty nappy
Or bandaging a grazed knee.

Continually handing out money
For this new thing or that,
At times giving all of my time
To a selfish little brat.

But there are the many golden days
When the tantrums have ended,
You bring me a present you made at school
And to me it is more than splendid.

Then you put your arms around my neck
And kiss me on the cheek,
The pure love and warmth I feel
Is all the present I seek.

Jack Ellis

My Dad

He was there when I was born, that bright September morn,
His face just beamed with joy, for I was his first boy.
But changing my dirty nappy, he wasn't quite so happy,
And crying mostly nightly, he couldn't take to lightly.

My later wanting potty, would often send him dotty,
And baby foods so thick, made him feel often sick.
Before I reached age five, he taught me to swim and dive,
And when I came to eight, he took me off to skate.

At ten he heard my wishing, and showed the art of fishing,
But when I got to fourteen, he genned me up on courting.
At sixteen leaving school, he called me a *B* fool,
'Stay till you pass your As, forget the *want work* craze.'

But landing on my feet, both he and mam were sweet,
He bought a motor bike, saying 'Ride it if you like.'
My twenty-first was great, the party his greatest treat,
'Now a man - you're not *my lad*, but remember, - I'm still your Dad.'

W Beynon

It Seems Like Only Yesterday. . .

It seems like only yesterday you bounced me on your knee
And we sat down together to eat our Sunday tea
You took me out to play football, taught me to ride a bike
Showered me with presents, gave me everything I liked
You sent me off to college, gave money so I could phone,
Always let me know I had a loving home.

It seems like only yesterday, I made you a Grandad
I could see by the smile upon your face you were really glad
You taught him how to ride his bike and be a footballer too
You really will now never know quite how much we all loved you.

It seems like only yesterday we came to visit you
And found your days of fatherhood were finally all through
Though we weren't there at the end we were glad it's true
That we had always had the chance to say we loved you.

Margaret Smythers

Parents

It's not that we think we know everything
It's just that we do know something
And we like to air our views from time to time
And really, where's the crime in that?

Daniel Hawthorne

On Moving Away
(For Simone)

I know now I have to rediscover
Living alone without your presence there.
We, who were so close to one another,
Who always found it interesting to share
The hopes and mishaps of each passing day.
The discords, disagreements that we had
No longer matter. I can only say
My memories are fond and I am glad
That we had the chance to be together
A full five years. But now it's time for you
To start again; a time to endeavour
To rebuild life and happiness pursue.
So I wish you the best and hope you note
That this is a sonnet your Father wrote!

Terence Jacob

Fatherhood

An angry bundle, small and red,
That's how you saw him first,
He'd no idea that fatherhood
Can't really be rehearsed.

He never dreamed you wouldn't know
Exactly what he'd need,
And, thought it often took a while
You'd usually succeed.

You would have moved the world for him,
He pulled your life apart,
Those freckles and that cheeky face
Played havoc with your heart.

You taught him all he'd need to know
And shared his hopes and fears,
You tried to stand him in good stead
For life in future years.

Although, throughout his teenage years,
He liked the easy life,
You saw how fast his outlook changed
The day he met his wife.

And now your heart is filled with pride,
How fast the years have flown!
Today he's independent
With a baby of his own.

Debbie Cowdry

My Pop

A puffing pipe, pipe puffing Pop.
Fine brown hair, with a bald patch on top,
Two thick beetle eye brows in line
Above blue eyes that sparkle and shine.
A nose that *The Schnoz* would admire,
Two lips that set Mum's heart on fire.

Huge hands that worked hard with a cause,
To make Toby my dear rocking horse.
A green fingered gardening guy,
Growing veg, flowers, and fruit, for a pie.

A connoisseur cook who connives
To ignore washing up, but derives
Such pleasure from making the tea,
For Mandy, and Mummy and me.

A soft slippered shuffling step,
That can change to a step full of pep
For a musical mood makes him move,
To awaken Wayne Sleep, who'd approve.
It's teatime, time for tea now, so stop,
Put your feet up, my pipe smoking Pop.

Marion Smith

Holliane

For the sweetest little girl in the world . . .

You melt me with your smile,
your big blue eyes
make it all worthwhile.
I feed you, I clothe you,
and proudly watch you grow,
I protect you from the world outside,
and love you more than you'll ever know.
I made you, and yet, you made me see,
I gave you life,
you give much more to me.

From the proudest Dad.

Anthony Greenwood

My Dad

Dad you were always one of the best,
Kind, generous, hard working too,
Now that you've gone to your eternal rest
I often think of you.

Today's high tech age seems like a dream
Compared to yours in a life of steam.
Working hard in all kinds of weather
As a family we pulled together.

Driving trains was your occupation,
To get there on time was the destination.
On your old push-bike away you sped
As you rode from home to the engine shed.

Gardening was how you spent your leisure,
Our back garden was such a treasure.
Flowers and vegetables all summer through
You gave them away as fast as they grew.

On Saturday's it was you, Mum and me,
Off to a film at the old Roxy,
Then afterwards Mum and I home at last,
Leaving you with your cronies for your usual glass!

Those were the days Dad!
We were happy and glad,
But time passes on for us all you see,
Now all that's left is a memory.

Barbara Colman

Dad

A young girl, she is always looking
For a man to share her life.
She goes through hell, hurt and pain,
Trouble, toil and strife.

If she stops and looks for a minute
Nothing is really that bad.
For turn around and he'll be there -
Forever loving Dad.

Of course, like Mum, he sometimes must
Turn about and give you a shove
In the right direction,
But of course it's all for love.

You're never too old for cuddles
Or even a little kiss.
For you are still Daddy's Little Girl
Even after wedded bliss.

Emma J Palmer

The Orphan

I've been dying to see my Father
Since I was a bundle of fun.
He died and became a stranger.
He went like the setting sun.
I grew, still dying to see him.
I mourned for want of a name,
For a Father to own with pleasure,
A Father to join in the game.

I have carried on fighting, enduring
The torments caged in my head,
The shame and the disappointment,
For I was as good as dead.
But now, on the eve of my seventieth,
I look at my Father's face
In the photograph at my bedside
And see in it grace upon grace:

For, no longer is he a stranger;
His good soul lives in his eyes.
I see in them, too, my own soul,
My own eyes with my own eyes.
And more! There's the sparkle of humour,
Compassion, a tolerant vein;
And I find I can laugh as he laughed,
With no derision or pain.

Fulfilment for me may follow:
While others triumphantly rise
To the peak, where I see them shining,
I reach, in hope, for the skies.

Margaret Smith

Father - Foremost Friend

To children there is nothing that a father cannot do
Broken toys and confidence are fixed with care and glue
Sunday mornings on the station bridge to watch the trains
Fishing trips and bike rides when it hardly ever rains

Years have passed - I'm older now than you were in those days
Distant are the memories of childhood's golden haze
But some things never really change as you all too well know
for who will get the call for help next time the fuses blow?

Mandy Smith

To Daddy

I woke again last night and asked Mummy where you are,
She says she doesn't really know if you are near or far.
She says she loved you once not very long ago,
But then the love began to die as I began to grow.
Sometimes I cry in bed at night, just wondering if you care;
Sometimes I hate this world you know, it really isn't fair.
At school the other Daddies come to take their children home;
But Mummy always comes for me, so I'm not left alone.
Sometimes I wish I knew you, other times I just don't care;
For when I'm ill, or when I'm sad, my Mummy's always there.
She often gets annoyed at me, and then can I look out;
Cause when she starts I run like mad to avoid her screams and shouts.
But I love her and I know that she loves me;
It's just I'm curious as to why I've got no Dad.
I'd really miss Mummy if she went away,
But you can't miss what you've never had.

Caroline Brown

My Dad

There was a man in my life from birth to marriage.
He nursed me in his arms, he held my hand.
This dear man wiped my tears, and we shared laughter,
Night-time stories, bedtime prayers.

There was not much money, though he worked so hard.
Christmas presents were lovingly handmade. A doll's dresser,
A puppet theatre, my own little table.
Many a game of Ludo or Snap we played on this.

Hand in hand, we walked over fields and cliffs.
Paddled in the sea, built sandcastles.
I see him now in his workshop, wearing his white apron, the big pocket
full of nails.
Repairing furniture, upholstering chairs, stuffing mattresses.

The day came when he *gave me away*,
Gave me away in marriage.
Then dear Dad, how thrilled he was, when
I presented him with his first Grandson.

Sadly the years took their toll, the time came to say goodbye.
How glad I am, I could hold his hand tight and say -
'I love you. Thank you, thank you for everything always.
God bless dear Daddy. I will never forget you.'

Peggy Buckett

A Sonnet: To My Daughter
(Born on May 10th 1945)

My *daughter* - born as wars in Europe end!
My wife and I had vowed: 'No children yet -
While mad destruction threatens all our fate,
And wolves of Fascism encircle us and rend -
The innocent: and weak; leaving us grow old!'

But passion's seeds are sown in spite of cold.
The bud expands and bursts through frozen soil.
We did not plan your coming in harsh times:
But, sweet coincidence, your birthday chimes -
With the ringing of the *Victory in Europe* bell!
And, erstwhile dialectician, I well recall:
The words of Heraclitus - that - 'From dire strife -
Comes *Joy*; and from dark death - springs radiant *Life*!'
And darling buds of May can blossom after all!

George Greening

The Visit

Timeless
I retread
My feet
In the yesterdays
Of my mind
And I are
There again
Running
Wind in my hair.

Timeless
I remember
My father
In the
Wonderful
Storehouse
Of memories
And I
Are there
Again
Coming
To see you.

Lin Legerton

Back Home

Hiding in the front room, I heard his key in the lock
The door was open, shut, and then the work boots wiped on mat
A belated return, delayed that night until well past seven o'clock,
But the chance was there for overtime so really that was that.

Springing from my domestic lair, I pounced on homecoming Dad,
This ritual evening ambush was our animated greeting,
He knew that all was well if he was pummelled by his lad
And surely missed the days when he received no playful beating.

For years I felt secure with this as part of my routine
And when this sporting clash was stopped I really can't recall,
Not the most gripping contest that the world has ever seen
But still I sense excitement racing with me down the hall.

Steve Woollard

Fathers Day Anthology

Our Father God gave us a pattern, and it's so very sad,
That still some Dads are wonderful, but some so very bad,
But real, true fathers are totally different breed
They seem to know instinctively their children's every need.

Listening, whilst the kiddies tell them all their hurtful woes,
From where they get their patience, goodness only knows!
They speak of brighter things, happier times ahead,
And tell them lovely stories, as they tuck them into bed.

While growing up, they're watching to help them all they can,
To guide them while they seek, for the one and only girl, or man,
Who will whisk them off light-heartedly, from his precious care,
Will wisdom then prevail? When they find a partner, their life to share.

Pray for the wisdom Fathers, it's a tragic world out there,
Teach your lovely children, to be honest, to love, to care,
Then we could defeat, that horrific growing trend to hate,
Before God brings down the curtain, and we find that it's too late.

F E Mullis

The Image of My Father

I was born into a father's mould,
and in your shape I grew;
self-engenderment I hadn't grasped,
uniqueness I never knew.

I was constantly reminded,
how much like you I did look;
and on more than one occasion,
for you I was mistook.

The mirror was my nightmare,
the destroyer of my self;
the place that I would hide from,
the foundation of my stealth.

In my fight for independence,
to be a person of my own;
I shaved my head and grew a beard,
and speedily left home.

But my ancestral trail I could not leave,
for within me you did dwell;
so my quest turned to my memory,
where thoughts of you did swell.

The loving Father who taught me right,
who showered me with grace;
the man that I looked up to,
with whom I shared a face.

Now when people say to me,
how much like my father that I am;
I smile at them and nod my head,
for I am an extremely lucky man.

Isn't it funny how an insult can grow,
into the greatest of all compliments.

Gary Ballard

The Job

I'd tuck them into bed and thrill to see
The sleepy souls that love had brought to me.
Little did I know, as I do now
The contradictions life would then allow,
And the pleasures and the problems there would be.

There were days of early childhood, all too few,
When minds, so young, were baffled by the new.
Then early school encounters, the progress made,
And unwelcomed influences that too often swayed
And lastly, the testing time of teenage point of view.

These problems I tackled as I should.
I made mistakes, and hoped they were understood.
For experience is a gift that can't be bought
Just as fatherhood's the skill that isn't taught.
And so the years were passed in doing what I could.

Life flows on, and all things fade away,
As did the caring days, and hours of play.
I've time in which to ponder, and perhaps to rue
The things not done and now too late to do.
Although I did the job I could, the only way!

Joe Rossiter

To Dad (Gone not Forgotten)

It's too late to say goodbye,
It's too late to wonder why.
God has took you to his side,
And many tears have we cried.
We thought you would stay forever
But forget you not we will never,
The memories will always stay
They cannot be taken away,
Regrets we have all ask why,
Why we could never say goodbye,
Little things we could have done,
But our Lord you still would have won.
Your time had come, you had to go,
And grief is all we live and know.
We know you're with our Lord above,
Filled with peace and filled with love.
Love you Dad, we always will,
And we know today our world will be still.
Memories of you will linger on,
And in our hearts you'll never be gone.

Kay Orme

The Novice

The man in my life
Never has had a wife,
Never had trouble and strife
From offspring of his own . . .

Never woken at night
To a babe in plight
Or been begged for sweets when the pocket's too light.
Reckons fathering is easy . . .

So to alter his thinking
And give him a peek
Into family life, just for a week,
My grandchildren came, all four . . .

For a week, each day,
He had them, his way.
It was harder than keeping his two dogs at bay.
He tried pleas, threats and rate for the job . . .

His body exhausted,
His temper depleted,
His cashflow deleted,
As a father he'll never succeed . . .

So he'll take on a grandad's role instead,
And hands them back when it's time for their bed . . .

Brenda Barry

My Special Dad

My Dad is quiet and kind,
The best you could ever find,
He always stays cool and calm
Whenever there's cause for alarm.

Whenever I have a nightmare
You can be sure he's always right there,
He dries all my tears
And listens to my fears.

I love to sit upon his knee
For a story to be read you see,
He always holds me very tight
And then I know everything's alright.

I'm lucky to have such a Dad,
It makes me feel really glad,
My Dad's very special to me
As everyone's Dad should be.

Eileen Everson

To Father-in-Law

Dear Father-in-Law, we admire your life so much,
With all the changes you have had to cope with.
You suffered the experiences of this century's wars
Managing to survive with undaunted fortitude.

When the doctors could not heal your poor leg,
They sought your permission for amputation.
You gave it bravely, saying you were glad to be rid of it.
You even kept up the spirits of your fellow patients.

The loss of limb did not dampen your zeal,
It seemed to make your body and mind stronger.
Now with crutches, frame and wheelchair
You manage to keep mobile in your own home.

Your personality is as vibrant as ever,
With the voice of kindness you speak right out -
We all know where we are with you,
You stand for justice and for truth.

So, dear Father-in-Law, as you soldier on
Battling against all the odds of this world,
Please know you are loved by all your family -
We are so very proud of you!

Doreen Hughes

Father's Joy

Like a rose-bud your petals unfolded
And in the centre of the bloom
A child as sweet as honey laid
Fluttering like a butterfly.

You have not been attended, nor cultivated.
You have shrivelled and withered with neglect.
But my child is full of love
And she is more than beautiful.

Tanya Gray

Dad

As yet I am a child
and I have my life to plan,

I hope that I can grow
and become a better man,

We had happy times
you and I,
But you walked out that day
without saying Goodbye,

When I grow up and have
a son of my own,

I'll guide him through life
until he is grown,

If you read this then hear
what I say,

I still love you Dad
why didn't you stay?

Lynn Barnes

From Out of This Backyard
(Father and Daughter)

Daddy, Daddy, please
Let's plant this tiny acorn
Because I learned today at school
That from tiny acorns grow big trees

Daughter, Daughter
What do you see?
We have no garden of flowers and trees
Just a small backyard of concrete and stone
We have no soil to make things grow

Daddy, Daddy, please
Make a garden for me!
So we can plant this acorn
And watch it grow into a tree

Daughter, Daughter, let's see
I'm not a gardener or a handyman
But I'll borrow a pick and shovel
And do the best I can
I will sweat and toil
To turn this concrete into soil

Daughter, Daughter, together we
Will plant this acorn
And we will see
If from out of this backyard
We can grow a great oak tree.

Kevin Cooper

Dear Dad

Dear Dad
I hope you're feeling better
I can't come and see you
So I'm writing you a letter

Mum says you're on a drip
And the food is really bad
An old man died next to you
So you're feeling very sad

When you had your op'
It went without a hitch
The surgeon did his best
But you think he dropped a stitch

I must end my letter now
I'm longing to visit you
I'll bring you my last sweet
I hope that you can chew

Oh, Mum pranged your car
I hope you won't be cross
Don't tell her I told you
Lots of love from Joss.

Joan M Littleworth

The Treasured Years

The nurse arrived before the dawn,
By half past six, the babe was born.
That little babe, turned out to be,
The happiest child, you'd ever see.
Before she learned, to speak a word,
She'd copy all the sounds she heard.

When she could speak, we were confused,
We'd never heard, some words she used.
Mumpf and *Dib-dib*, were but two.
We learned to used them, and still do.
Mum bakes *Victoria Mumpf* for me,
And I like *Dib-dibs* dunked in tea.

She had a *trike* when she was small,
And loved to *piddle* it up the hall.
She had a little phantom friend,
With whom she'd play for hours on end.
Beebum was with her constantly
He'd sit beside her during tea.

She told us things he did and said,
At night she'd tuck him into her bed.
Her friend, *Beebum* didn't go away,
Till her brother was old enough, to play.
As they got older, we couldn't share their fun,
Therefore we planned to have another one.

My wife had insisted, that she wouldn't mind the pain,
So once more, after fifteen years, our lives began again.
Those joyful years returned once more, as rich or richer than before.
Now after three years and a score, we're too old to have some more.
But thankful for the forty years of pleasure, that we've had.
Life would have seemed quite fruitless, if I hadn't been their Dad.
R Baker

One Tiny Voice

I am a small face pressed
to the window
waiting for my Dad
he said he would come
cause he told my Mum
so I know I musn't be sad.

I have a small heart beating
inside me
waiting for my Dad
for it's Sunday today
and he's come to play
cause I am his little lad.

I have a small hand held
very tightly
tenderly by my Dad
but the hour races by
and I know I will cry
with the limited time that we had.

I am a small soul trying
to capture
the sweet song of yesterday
and I will be good
for I promised I would
if only my Daddy would stay.

Hilary Malone

Fishing with Father

Who am I? Who should have been your first born son,
The heir. You have not learnt this century's rules
Yet, I think you should have been born elsewhere,
And in some other time.

You taught me how to gut rabbits, at the age of four,
But while their skins were still on I used
To take my little cart
And push them around the kitchen floor
Like babies in a pram.

And later, on cold October mornings,
Out in the fields with our dogs and your gun,
I helped you flush woodcock from the hedgerows
And watched the little rabbits run,
Before you shot them.

I had such tenderness for those rabbits, I picked them
Gently out the mud, and held them so tight to my body,
They stained my coat with their warm blood.

You went and bought me a fishing rod,
And we went fishing by the sea,
And in the wind I prayed to God,
To turn this she into a he.

But it didn't happen, and the fish I caught
I dropped,
You had to pick them up for me
And dash their brains out on the rocks.

I daydreamed when we went bird-watching,
I would not eat rabbits in a stew,
I tried to be the son you really wanted,
But I was only a girl, Dad.
And I think the real failure was you.

Emma Morgan

One Day the Angels Came . . .

Dedicated to my Dad who passed away on the 18th March 1980.
Forever in my thoughts.

When I was young you read to me,
Stories of dreamy lands and faraway places,
Clouds of candy floss,
And pretty girls in ribbon and laces.

As I grew older,
You taught me what was wrong and right,
And told me not to be afraid,
Of things that go bump in the night.

You taught me how to be polite,
And what was good and bad,
And taught me how lucky I was,
For all the nice things I had.

But then one day the angels came,
And took you faraway,
For they saw, you were tired,
And knew you couldn't stay.

First I really hated God,
How could he take my Dad,
To take him to another world,
And leave me feeling sad.

Now I realise he was being kind,
He saw you needed rest,
And to take you up to Heaven,
He knew it would be best.

I'll always have my thoughts,
And memories of you,
And I know that you are with me,
In everything I do.

So before I lay down to sleep,
I pray to God above,
And ask him to take care of Dad,
And give him all my Love.

Vivian T Mabbutt

My Dad

I wish I knew who he was - my Dad.
What he did?
You see, my mum had a fling in the war.
She no but a kid.
Oh, she loved him alright - my Dad.
A GI over here.
Handsome in uniform and so free,
With nylons so sheer.
Whilst bombs dropped she and - my Dad
Cuddled and kissed.
Then he was sent back to the States.
Very sadly missed.
My Mum wrote and told him - my Dad.
A baby they'd made.
Letter returned - not known at this place.
No forthcoming aid.
My Gran went berserk at my Mum and - my Dad.
Called her a whore and a tart.
There was no notice taken at all.
Of Mum's broken heart.
The disgrace was hard to bear - my Dad.
My Mum had to fight.
To keep me, to feed me so well.
Money was tight.
But we survived without you - my Dad.
But I still want to know
Would you have loved me - not left me.
Why did you go?

Sandra Emmerson

One in a Million

My Dad is a banker and he has been for thirty years,
But if you asked him now, he'd not advice it for a career.
The banking principles have changed since he was a young lad,
Bankers used to help their clients with the problems that they had.

But now the bank is just a profit-making company,
Every time it does a little job it asks for a huge fee
It likes to charge high mortgage rates to put people in debt,
The bank is a place where you never get quite what you expect.

My Dad always worries and is concerned about these things,
He does not like to see the unhappiness that the bank brings
He really wants to help people in any way he can,
Because he is a very caring and loving sort of man.

But there are other things about my Dad that you should know,
Like he is a wizard at making creamy mashed potato
But other than that my Dad simply cannot cook a thing,
And those that know him well, know he definitely cannot sing.

But under those few weaknesses there is a heart of gold
(Just don't remind him he's greying and quickly getting old).
He's kind, he's considerate, and he's friends with everyone,
My Dad is special because he's one in a million.

I've written these words so that everyone can really see
That my Dad is the best Dad that there could possibly be.
He embarrasses me sometimes and his jokes are quite mad
But despite this I love him just because he is my Dad.

Rachel Evans

A Matter of Luck

Every child deserves a good father
But alas what can they do
When it needs a sensible mother
To choose the right father for you.

Fathers come in all shapes and sizes
All colours religions and creeds.
Yet the good ones have something in common
They all care for their children's needs.

A good father can be rich or famous
Or as poor as the poorest church mouse.
He may work in those far distant places
Or simply just tend to the house.

If you are lucky and have a good father
Then for once give some thought to his pleasure
Cherish and love him, heed what he says,
A good father is someone to treasure.

J Calvert

Dads Day - Fun Day

To be a Dad
I hope you know
How it's done?
You'll find a Mum
Who'll have some fun
And make a little one.

You'll find a Mum
Who'll suffer little brats
With rashes.
Who'll change the nappies
Pretend she is happy,
And will not up and run.

Now you the Dad are sad
It's such a racket
She takes your pay packet.
No night without a fight,
You wish you did a flight
And possibly you're right.

It was such fun doing it!
Until you hit it!
And became a Dad.
Now it is very sad -
You've got a growing lad
Who never listens to his Dad.

His sister who is fat
And loves a little cat.
She never talks to Dad.
She'll soon be up and at it!
Out looking for a lad -
To make a woeful Grandad.
A MacGábann

Dad and Me

See the picture:
A daughter and her Dad
So happy
So proud.
Why
When I love you so
Do I not allow my own pain
To show;
For never having forgiven
Myself
And just
Letting you know.

Marlene Morris

Sad Songs No More

Life croons with our ballads
'Tis a playground of song
But sometimes the sad songs paint the characters grey
Once you were born
Tears coloured the dawn
Leaving room in my heart where the piper must play

Which door do I open
Which ballad do I sing
Which path along parenthood do I decide
The journey of parents
Is all life has meant
My child is the pawn my future has lent

Hope trickles through streams
Pain stagnates in pools
Love surges like a river soothing the wounds of my child
We picture our shrine
Where our beacon must shine
Painted with love in the colour of time

'Tis a song of a child
A gift wrapped in life
A gift from the heart which the piper must tune
The message may sigh
The words make me cry
A song for a Father in the ballad of June

On this special June morn
There's a tear in my heart
The love of a child flutters in through the door
Words spelt from the heart
Upon a Fathers' Day card
Nay shall I listen to those sad songs no more
David Bridgewater

Constable

The constable moves slowly in a measured way
The constable moves slowly along the high street on a busy day
Slowly and surely, surely and slow, quietly watching the ebb and flow
The constable is caring, the constable is kind
The constable is confident he can battle against crime

The constable moves slowly with hands behind his back
Truncheon tucked inside his jacket, that is a matter of fact
The constable has a strap tucked underneath his chin
Children love to see his helmet and, underneath, his big grin

The constable is handsome, people love him so
Up the Edge, along the Bays, and down the Bish he goes
Looking out for trouble, prostitutes or thieves
Looking out for children who may be being teased

I love a special constable, his name is *Dad* to me
He was always popular at Paddington Green you see
People loved to meet him, people loved to chat
He loved to tell them *the little tale* and pat them on their back

He never did anybody any harm, Bill or Ben or Bob
He did not want promotion, he just *got on with the job.*

Margaret Bennett

Untitled

A Father is someone precious, whom we should love so much,
He guides us through the path of life
With a helping hand, and a special touch.
A gentle word, kind thought or deed,
Someone to cheer us along life's way.
He tries to teach us, and show us his care
So that when we need him, he is always there.
A Father's love is dear to us, just like a mother's too,
From the moment we are born, and while we grow up
It surrounds us daily, so tender and true.
So to all Father's out there, wherever you may be,
We want to express our love,
And say *thank you* for just being a Dad
And for all the good times, which we remember we had.

Gladys Luckin

Fathers Day

There was a young man called Arthur
A wise and intelligent father.
Proud of his home, his wife and boys
This was his life and all his joys.
But sadness shrouded his home one day
His wife had left; took the boys far away.
So now he's back with mum to stay
This wise and intelligent Father.

The phone would ring and it's 'Hello Dad
Wish you were here, this house is so sad,
We miss the fun we all had together
Football, tennis, snooker seems gone forever.'
The joy of hearing his lad on the phone
Made Fathers' Day, as he thought of home.
'Don't worry my boy, I still love you all dearly
It's still grand to be a Father.'

Lilian Ware

Love is Not Allowed Farther

I loved my Father.
I think he loved me.
It was very hard to tell.
They rowed all the time, I know not why.
Such a sad time to tell.
The bitterness would start.
My Mother would gather us up out the door we would go.
Father would sit alone.
My heart would sink for him, deeper still.
I loved my Father.
I wished I was allowed to get near to him.
Maybe some day I hopefully will.

Maxine Davison

Dad

You are the greatest Dad
Because you're always there
You help me when I'm down
You care when I am sick
You can not give me
Gifts galore
Because you are not rich
But Dad you are the greatest
Because you give me more
More than money
Could ever buy
You give me your love
I am rich.

Margaret Hickman

A Blessing in Disguise

It is such a joy to be a Dad,
Sometimes happy sometimes sad,
My daughter is such a joy,
Followed by our baby boy.

Those early days could be so tough,
But I could never have enough,
Heartaches often tinged our way,
But I wouldn't change a single day.

I would have to work away sometimes,
A loneliness in my heart I'd find,
The weekend at last would come around,
Home once more where love abounds.

Through my children's teenage years,
My daughters love dispelled my fears,
How could I have ever guessed,
With such a gift I'd been blessed.

As I travel on through life,
I was blessed to find my wife,
My son would listen very intent,
Our advise he said was time well spent.

Now my young ones are mature,
The more I look the more I'm sure,
Of all the gifts bestowed I see,
Our family mean the world to me.

Now our children at last have grown,
They have families of their own,
I see our lifeblood passing on,
A precious gift when I am gone.
Jim Wilson

That Day

Illuminative face of wonder before me
You are my child, welcome.
Blood is still upon your brow.

Sweet scent of jasmine wafts under my nose
As if for a moment we are in India,
On a summers night, or is it an Angel
Leaving a sign to let me know - then it is gone.

My child
It is you in my arms, bless you for you have chosen,
You have chosen me as your father.

It was such a touching moment
Then before I knew it, you were taken from me.

How a scent can hold such memories.
Whenever I smell Jasmine now
I think of the nights in India
With the sky ablaze with stars,
I think of the love from which you came from,
I think of the Angels,
And I think of you.

Séan Whyte

Father, Do You Know Me?

I wonder, dear Daddy, if you see you as I do,
Older and wiser, all knowing in life,
Happily married, child, house and car,
Money and twenty years with a loving wife.

I ponder, dear Daddy, do you see me struggle,
To make of myself what life's made of you,
I strive for your wealth, your time and your love,
But you wander on past and look me right through.

I expect, my dear Daddy, it's hard being a Father,
A provider, supporter, in control of each day,
But as hours pass, all grows more distant,
Be careful, my Father, that we don't slip away.

I know now, dear Daddy, just what is important,
Have us, and want us, or we will be none,
Oh so important is family bonding,
Please let three together join into one.

Sarah Cheetham

My Father, the Soldier

Your photographs show a handsome strong soldier,
You travelled far in defence of your country.
I did not know you then
For I was born just after the war.

I wonder if it was difficult in those post-war years.
You must have missed your comrades and the confines of duty,
To settle down into a civilian world
Putting down roots with a wife and children.

It was a long time before war's business was finished.
You actively helped to settle the more unfortunate -
Those who made it back home in the years after war's end.
Your keen support also helped the reunions to survive.

Looking back, I remember what a kind father you were,
Teaching us skills with our bikes and balls,
Buying our first records to play on the wind-up gramophone,
Life was so simple then.

I regret the heartaches I must have caused you,
As I grew up into the difficult years.
I surely tried your patience to its very limit,
But somehow we came through it all.

The years have gone on rolling by,
Now you have become a Great-Grandfather,
Still actively helping in the community.
Father dear, we all think the world of you.

Gladys Hughes

Fathers Day

They are there for us in all shapes and size
We heed their word believing them to be wise
Gentle and understanding of our many needs
Will swiftly and firmly chastise us
When we get into mischievous deeds
Little girls can twist them around their fingers
For he cannot resist their charm
He knows he must protect her
Shielding her from harm
Little boys he will teach to grow into a man
Teaching them everything that he can

There to soothe our troubles
When in our young lives we often get in
Staunch, Honest and Loving
There is only one of him
Often the one who helps us ride the pitfalls of life
He stands united by our side
There is an aura about him we look up to him in awe
Teaches us right from wrong so we will know the score

Tired after a long working day
But still finds the time with us to play
Maybe he is not the best at sport not every father can be
Still I know no matter where I am he will always be there for me
Once a year Fathers' Day arrives
Him a present I will lovingly give
Be it slippers or socks or a shaving lather
He will always be our loving *Father*

Vera Witt

Just for a Moment

You lay motionless, sterile room covering you with unknown fear,
eyes wide with morbid anticipation,
the rhythm of your heart so profound,
Father, I lost you

Just for a moment

I felt lonely, then anger took over completely,
hope for the future took wing
on feathered clouds, tearful, as only grief can bring
Father, I lost you

Just for a moment

Nearby lovers still embrace with desire, bodies bare,
a solitary blackbird flew by the window with its soulful stare.
Outside spruce trees moved, restless in the winnowing wind, as
I lost you

Just for a moment

Gently I found you again, deep within my secret heart
where love hides and rage subsides,
Dear Father I was unprepared for the isolation, the sadness when
I lost you

Just for a moment.

Derene O L Rowe

Dad's Love

You were the first man, that I ever saw,
The first love, that I ever had,
No one could ever take your place,
'Cos you're my own, beloved Dad.

Who was there first, whenever I fell,
Who wiped away all that blood,
Who fell about laughing, whenever I,
Would come home all covered in mud.

Who was there first, when I had my bad dreams,
Who worried when I was sick,
Who made me a cot, for all of my dolls,
And made me stilts out of sticks.

Who championed me, when Mum got mad,
At the silly things I'd done,
Who was the one, had to wipe away tears,
At the slightest prize, I'd won.

Who was the one, who showed all his love,
No matter, whatever I did,
Who laughed so hard, tears rolled down his face,
When from my Mother, I hid.

Who was the one, who couldn't say goodbye,
The day I first left home,
Who was the first, to visit me,
So I wouldn't feel alone.

Who filled my world with sunshine,
And chased away, all the rain,
Always worked his fingers to the bone,
So all of us could gain.

There's all kinds of Fathers, all kinds of Dad,
But I had the best one, a girl ever had . . .

Pamela Marling Ferguson

Why Did God Call You so Soon

Hello Dad just wanted to say,
That little baby was your Grandson on the way,
His hair is brown, his eyes are too,
Some people say he looks quite like you.
He's tall for his age, now twenty months,
He talks quite a lot and says Grandad too,
Unfortunately though he can't say it to you.
Oh why did God call you so soon?

Hilary Chaplin

Father - Where Art Thou?

Where art you now?
went crashing out of my life
like a foaming, bolting horse
and galloped away to where?

Oh Father it was so long ago
that you've missed me age and grow
out of needing you,
Yes, that's almost true.

Perhaps it was for the best
perhaps from God it was a test
of my inner strength, yet
your crime? You liked a bet
just my luck - to get a Father
that bolted before it all got started.

Bitterness now seems so pointless,
just like a poem about a disappearing
Father, well hope
you're alright, on this poignant day.

Paul Cornell

A Father's Love

Being a Father isn't easy
I've three girls - aged seven to ten
The things they ask amuse me
About the facts of life - often

They sit and watch my reaction
I'll be as honest as I can
Sometimes a little over-protective
More so than any other Dad

Their Mum she died a year ago
Life up to then's been kind
I try to make them understand
To give them peace of mind

Their future won't be easy
No one knows what lies ahead
Your life on earth is precious
'Cause you're a long time dead

I tell them life is what you make it
Be good, be kind and strong
Don't be tempted to ever stray
And then you can't go wrong

Honesty comes from the heart
Believe me I should know
The day their mother died
I let my feelings show

At home we have an understanding
Even father's sometimes feel down
Don't hide your feelings ever
Show your love - it works I've found
M E Wickett

Our Daddy

Our Daddy is one in a million - that's true
He's our big brother, friend and confidant too.
He joins in our fun and games so happily
And our play-fighting especially is a sight to see!
With three of us against him you'll always find -
He comes off the worse but he never seems to mind.
He teaches us the difference between right and wrong,
He has impressed this upon us all our life long

Our Daddy often comes out with us on our bikes,
And in summer he takes us for wonderful hikes.
Football in the park - swimming too.
He always finds something great for us to do.
We think he's good at so many different things
(although we cover our ears whenever he sings!)
He can take a joke and pulls our legs too.
He repairs all our toys so they're good as new.

Our Daddy has always made it clear
That with him around we've nothing to fear.
If we have any worries we talk them through
And he cheers us up if we're feeling blue
He helps with school-work and gives us the encouragement we need
And lets us know he's very proud of us indeed.
He gives us our freedom, but you can also be sure
He protects us and guides us, so we feel very secure.

We may only be children but we're wise enough to know -
Our Daddy is *the best* and we all love him so.

To *the best* with all our love
Martyn, Sophie and Katie

Julie Hancox

Father, Dear Father

Father, dear Father, what can I say,
You met and married my Mother,
One fine summer day.
I was four years old at the time,
But it didn't matter,
You were my Father, I your daughter.

Father, dear Father, what can I say,
My Mother died in a mental home,
One cold January day,
I was alone at the time,
But it didn't matter,
You were my Father, but you went away.

Father, dear Father, what can I say,
You met and married another,
One fine September day,
We were meant to meet for lunch,
But it didn't matter,
You exchanged me for a honeymoon.
A new wife for an old daughter.

Father, dear Father, what can I say,
You decided to emigrate,
One dark winter day,
With a smile and a wave,
Twelve thousand miles you sailed.
Taking your family, you left me behind.

Father, dear Father, what can I say,
My life has been good,
And the seasons still change.
Sometimes it snows, sometimes it rains.
I get letters and cards,
Saying all that you do,
But none of them are ever signed by you.

Harrison Kahn

Fatherhood (Before and After)

Conception takes place and you're on your way,
Then for nine months you await the big day,
That day arrives and you are the newborn son,
Away from the safety of your Mum's warm tum,
You change from a young baby to a young boy,
You are your Mum and Dad's pride and joy,
Gradually you become older day by day,
And are taught to behave in a masculine way,
Then it's play-school time and off you go,
To make new friends for an hour or so,
Then education time arrives and it's all for real,
You experience lessons and your first school meal,
Some years later you leave to start your new career,
But you'd rather sit in pubs and ponder with your beer,
Eventually you settle down and when you're both quite sure,
You decide to begin a family and the cycle starts once more,
You both attend the classes and learn of what's to come,
Maybe you'll have a little girl or maybe a little son,
The special day comes up and your baby has arrived!
You pick it up and hold it close, filled with joy and pride,
Armed with your camera you take some snaps for everyone to see,
An album is made and you show off your baby, be it a he or a she,
One day you hear a pitter-patter as you open up a door
Your baby is behind you and crawling across the floor,
Being a Dad is pretty hard work, as soon you will come to know,
Your little baby wears you out as you watch it grow and grow,
When looking after your little person, you'll sometimes get no rest,
But when this little person is an adult, you'll know you've done your
best . . .

Stephen Norris

Ode for Fathers Day

This is a rhyme about my *Dad*,
'Tis Fathers' Day - of this I'm glad. . .
We country folk, do much revere:
Our *Dads*, because they are so dear.

He is always working about the farm,
Tending the animals - keeping them from harm.
He cares for us children, and gives us the best,
From dawn to dusk, with little rest.

'Tis on a Market day we feel so proud;
Smart with flat cap, and jacket loud,
He takes us around, and tells us tales:
Showing us the animals that are in the sales.

We love our dear *Dad*, and wish him well,
The Church will even ring a bell -
Good wishes and happiness we will bring,
As his praises, for always, we shall sing.

Kay Fleming

Thanks Dad

F or being fun to have around,
A nd ever there for me,
T rusting, caring, sharing your love,
H elping me on my way,
E ager to listen to my plans,
R easonable, when I'm not,
S teadfast, honest, gentle, and strong,
D reaming my dreams with me,
A lways ready to give your time,
Y our strength is all I need.

So on your day with love I say,
Once again thank you Dad.

Hazel Collins

Accepting

When will I accept you're gone
The memories hurt
Seeing your life slip past in a whisper
A crumpled heap on a hospital bed
Death rang out from every corner
I thought I'd seen it all till I saw you
My memory bank won't accept
The nightmare of those few days
The man that was is was
Goodbye Daddy, my only Daddy.

Cate Arculeo

The Real (and the Bell)

There once was a pub where laughter sang
Like ricochets along the walls,
Jollity and festivity high lords of the land,
Opening, until the lone bell rang,
Signal of the evening's climatic end.
. . . At lunchtimes my father would take me along
Would buy me a coke or lemonade,
Lift me onto a stool, where I would sit and read
My weekly comic page one to thirty-two
(A contented child)
Munching on the artificial flavour -
Of a packet of crisps
While he had a pint of best and with his mates
A chat, a jest . . .
Well, now it's gone!
Long since closed for business,
Replaced by a Saddlers I believe.
Dad's gone too, leaving memory in his wake.
Things change, they always do and always will,
Change catches up with each of us,
On occasion reverting to hard slam tackles
To land you on your believed individual face.
As you become older, wear, grey,
You miss childhood amusement,
Learn to deal with social abusement,
Is this the real, or is it only pretence, a fake?
. . . There once was a pub, now gone
. . . There once was a child, now grown
. . . There once was a man . . .
(And the bell rang).

Marlon Dwane Woodward

Thank You Dad

Thank you Dad for being you
And teaching me what to do,
Helping me in every way
To be a good citizen today.
You have always been kind and good
And have always understood
When I have a problem or worry
You have always solved it for me.

In the days when I was young
You came out in the sun
And we did tennis play
In the sun on a Summer's day.
Then some days in the car
With the children and with Ma
We would go to the sea
And play on the beach merrily,
Building castles, paddling too,
Oh so many things to do.
And you enjoyed the fun
With the children who had come.

Thank you Dad for what you are
You are the very best Pa.
And thank you Dad for being you
And helping me to know what to do.

Jean M Webster

Who'd be a Father?

If you don't get up soon my lad
I'll kick you out of bed,
and turn that awful music off
it goes right through my head.

The noise has shattered all the windows,
the dog is wearing Gran's ear plugs,
and Uncle's teeth are chattering
in the bathroom mugs.

The cat has gone demented,
it's sitting in the cage
with Jo the crosseyed budgie
who's in a frightful rage.

The fish is swimming backwards,
the hamster's fled in fright,
so turn that flippin' *music* off
or you and me'll fight.

Doreen Dean

Fathers Day

On Fathers' Day
all over the land.
Beautiful cards
on fireplaces stand.

Portraits of Dad
by a child carefully drawn.
Delivered by hand
at day's early dawn.

Big shiny cards
from a child who has grown.
Telephone calls
from the ones far from home.

It's so lovely to know
that some things never alter.
These tributes to Dads
from a son or a daughter.

Dorothy Dawson

Goodbye Dad

Eyes brim full of useless tears,
Remembering my childhood years.
Your special sweet affinity,
No longer here to comfort me.

I miss the laughter that we shared,
Wish I'd said how much I cared.
A black hole full of emptiness,
Devours my mind and leaves unrest.

A vision of your smiling face,
Fills my mind with gentle grace,
I never thought you'd ever die,
Regret I couldn't say goodbye.

My life force fades away from me,
Without your strength and company.
For you are gone away from here,
Eyes brim full of useless tears.

Jane E Desforges

A Sons Friend

You are the man of silent strength,
The person to whom I rely.
Whose words are soft when things go wrong,
And tough when my ego gets too high.

You are the man who taught me to fix a puncture,
The man who's oil and tools I constantly borrow.
And who's advice, now I am older,
I finally follow.

The list of things that you have done,
Would pass the moon and leave our solar system.
So all I can say, is '*Thank you Dad.*'
The best friend, a son could ever have.

A L Barlow

A Father's Pride

I pick him up so gently
This newborn son sublime,
A face just like a cherub
It melts this heart of mine,
Tiny hands and tiny toes
Hair as soft as silk,
I snuggle him close to my chest
And feel his small heart beat,
Gazing upon this tiny form
I feel a Father's pride,
Overwhelmed with emotion
And happiness I cried,
This tiny babe so perfect
Has brought with him much joy,
So long it seems I've waited
For a son, my baby boy.

Muriel Cooper

Super Dad

Are we going fishing Dad?
The rain's held off so far.
I'll make a pack of sandwiches
If you will bring the car.

Are we going to football Dad?
They're playing very near.
Our local team that's done so well,
We must give them a cheer.

Are we going for a walk Dad?
It's not too cold today.
We can have a good old chat
And a laugh along the way.

Yes son, I'll go with you
To do the things you say.
We'll spend some time together
Each and every day.

Gillian Thomson

What is a Dad

A Dad is the one pacing back and forth
Looking quite worried and coy
Waiting for news of the happening
Is it a girl or a boy

He's the one who expects all the praises
For that sweet little tot in the pram
Strutting about and explaining
A clever old fellow I am

He's the one who goes out in the morning
Leaving the rebels to Mum
And the one who says 'Had a good day Mum?'
As she clears up the toys and the drum

He's the one who looks after the engine
With train set spread all around
While the nibs hang around for a look in
As Dad stretches out on the ground

He's the one who is patiently waiting
When he knows he must lay down the law
As the nights out get later and later
And he paces the bedroom floor

He's the one who stands proud at the wedding
Wrinkles of joy on his face
Though his finances now have been strangled
He bears it with heavenly grace

But through all the trials, the joy, and the tears
The happy times linked with the bad
We know they will always respect him
Their strict but most lovable Dad
C Hall

Dad, do you Remember

Dad, do you remember when we children all were young
(Your back was firm and straight then, your limbs were lithe and strong)
How you could lift up two of us, both hanging on one arm,
Rejoicing in the strength that would keep us all from harm?

And, Dad, do you remember how much you used to tease
On Sunday walks in Spring, hanging chocolate bars on trees
And how you used to smile at our looks of pleased surprise,
With what delight you laughed at the questions in our eyes?

Oh, and Dad, do you remember those glorious Mays
When you marshalled your forces to make beanstick forays
And when in the warm sunshine you found us all reading
You called up your troops to do battle at weeding?

Do you remember, Dad, your special apple tree
In the middle of the garden and your numinous decree
To banish those partaking of (to curb lust of the eyes)
Forbidden fruit of Eden, your own sweet paradise?

Now, watching mother tend her flowers
Do you grieve for happy hours
In your quarter-acre spent
Growing veg to pay the rent?

The scarlet buzzer on the wall
Does it recall to you at all
Your ringing in the dawn
Bringing mother with a yawn,
To unlock the kitchen door?

Do you remember this no more?

Well, you can take your ease now, your duties all have ceased.
Our own *Abou-Ben-Adhem*, whose tribe has much increased!

Shirley H Ford

Young at Heart

My Dad is nearly eighty-one
And still has quite a lot of fun.
He discos all the night away,
At skittles - you should watch him play.
Dad paints in oils, or reads a book,
He'll garden, shop, keep house and cook.
All through the years, he's made me glad
And proud - that he's my caring Dad.

Diana H Adams

Dad Rest in Peace

Dad we didn't say goodbye,
Before on the wings of an angel you did fly.
But in my heart you will always be,
And the memories we shared will comfort me.
Your tears were not wasted,
Your work was worthwhile,
On my face you can still bring a smile.
Your words were full of wisdom,
Love and kindness too,
Rest in peace dear Dad,
Dear Dad I love you.

V Eastwood

Mum Works on Saturday

The day starts at 8.30 sharp
Breakfast bowls heaped
Nice and full.
An hour on your knee
In front of TV
And off to the pool
For a swim.

When I swam my first width
I just stared at your face
'Come on son, come on.'
With thumbs in the air
And encouraging glare
Your hand patted me
At the edge.

Egg sarnies are a must
On Saturday.
Followed by a stint on the Hornby.
A walk in the park
We play until dark
Do we miss Mum?
Not likely!

Alison Deare

Dad

Don't know where the time's gone Dad
Or how I've seen it through
'Cause not one minute of a day goes by
Without me missing you
They say all wounds are healed by time
So I guess it must be true
And it's a fact that I don't cry as much
As I used to do
But I can still see your face
Those mischievous, sparkly eyes
I can hear your voice, smell your pipe
And then I realise
You are not here, and the warmth of a tear
Threatens to break free
You are not here, Daddy so dear
You are not here with me
And as the healer of wounds slips by and by
It's easier to think of you and not cry
But in my heart there is always a sigh
And a sadness it just cannot deny
For there is a place there that is yours
And whatever the passing of time may bring
It will be there waiting for you
To fill it once again

Lynda Bailey

A Walk in the Ark

Shem, Ham and Japeth were three brothers
They were sons of Noah and begat many others.
One day the family was down in the dumps -
The animals were starting to give them the hump.
There weren't any problems getting to sleep -
A daily task was counting sheep.
'I can't take any more - it's all too much!'
Said Shem, 'I feel so out of touch.'
'You can't complain - you come out quite well'
Said Japeth, 'You've got no sense of smell!'

'What about me?' came the voice of Ham
'I thought it was a good job being the *Ice Man.*
Don't talk to me about penguins and polars,
I'm sick to the back teeth - up to my molars!'
The brothers hadn't noticed the extent of the tension
Spreading through the Ark and needing intervention.
It was obvious that everyone had had all they could take
It was time for them all to have a break.
So they put their heads together and came up with a plan
To do something special for their Old Man.

They decided to heal up all the rifts
By presenting him with gifts.
'Oh, you're too kind,' said Noah, his voice filled with elation
As his descendants lined up for the presentation.
His sons, grandsons and great-grandsons too,
Watched him open the presents two by two.
'Shoes?' he said, feeling a parcel. 'Very nice - mock crocks,
And you can never have too many pairs of socks. . .
Some fishing gear, a jumper and a trimmer for the lawn -
D'you know, I think this Fathers' Day business could catch on!'

Angela White

The Restaurant

They chose a table by the door,
But found it was too draughty.
So they chose a table by the fire
And ordered from a list.

The waiter came, but spilt some soup;
Behaviour not too crafty!
'Just wipe it up and bring the bill!'
An irate lady hissed.

The children ordered steak and chips,
Their Father ordered salmon;
He asked his wife what she preferred;
She said she'd like some gammon.

The meal was slow; took half-an-hour,
A fact they did not mention.
Then a picture hanging on the wall
Attracted their attention.

They ate their meal, enjoyed it well,
Then set off in a hurry.
'We'll come again,' their Father said
'But next time I'll have curry.'

P Bradwell

Paterfamilias

Stage one.
'Tell me a story, then I'll go to sleep.
Tell me a story.
Help me to count the sheep.'
Daddy!

Stage two.
Homework!
There you sit, brow furrowed,
Applying knowledge from your days of naval gunnery
To my problems of Euclid and Pythagorus.
Good old Dad!

Stage three.
'I promise I'll be home like Cinderella
Before the clock strikes twelve.'
There you stand in the doorway,
Waiting for your one ewe lamb.
Good old Pop!

Stage four.
The music swells,
And we walk the length of the aisle together.
Now you stand aside
Proud, dignified.
Dear Father!

Stage Five.
Grand-paterfamilias!

Caroline Ross

The Search for an Unknown Father

A mission to search,
search and find,
and when I find you?
well,
when you see me,
you'll know,
once you see my face
you'll know -
resemblance runs deeper than blood
across my long time dry cheek,
just as I found out,
you too will be found
and when I find you
we'll capture those lost times,
we'll form that Father and Son relationship,
we'll blame and punish
but end together at the boundary of love.
Even though you neglected me
I will find you,
together with part of myself
that I've never yet found,
because of you I don't know
what a father is,
only that he is a man,
that left me
so that I could spend my entire life
searching for him.

D A Lowe

A Loving Dad

Dad the things that you have done,
To help us when we were young,
Helping us with building blocks,
And lots of little things like that,
Rocking us on your knee,
While reading us our stories,
And now that we are all grown up,
You're still there with your love and care,
When we need your help, or advice,
You're there and treat us all so nice,
At times you look so stern and tough,
But Daddy dear you can't kid us,
Because we know deep down inside,
You're just one big and loving,
Softie Dad.

Jennifer Williams

Always

Always in the background
Solid as a tree
Letting me branch out in life
Not holding on to me . . .
Standing in the backdrop
You are always there
Helping me with all my needs
Knowing that you care . . .
I always will remember
The way you dried my tears
Held my hand along the way
Banishing my fears . . .
Always you are backstage
Waiting just to see
Should I need a helping hand
Branching out to me . . .
Always in my own backyard
Forever and a day
The branch will never shatter
All the memories will stay . . .
You will always be my hero
Always be my guiding star
Dearest Father, my best friend
Gently watching from afar . . .

Margarette L Damsell

To my Daughters - Love Dad

When I was young, barely a lad
I thought one day you'll be a Dad
A little lass upon your knee
Not one, but two or even three.
The years have passed, so full and plenty
And then behold your lad was twenty
With many girls I happed to pass
Yet found my own true love at last
First Linda came, then Viviane too
My wife, the pain that she went through
When troubles came they said please don't look sad
Cheer up, you are the world's best Dad
Then poor Mum was very ill
And Dad, her role he had to fill
He acted both as friend and waiter
They lived on beans, jelly and tater
And when at last they went to bed
'Twas Dad who patted each one's head
They said the fun has not begun
Let's go and visit dear old Mum
In bed they told her such a tale
My confidence began to pale
Of burnt, black bread and smelly stew
Oh dear! The trials the girls went through
Then one day, at home our Mum arrived
Her heart went cold when all she spied
She grinned and said I always knew
That Dad would help and see us through
So no I don't feel half as bad
You see I'm just another Dad.

Cyril Saunders

My First Fathers Day

I took my wife to the maternity hospital,
She was shouting in so much pain,
'I hate you for this,' she said, to me
'You won't get me here again.'

I tried to go with her to the labour ward,
But she said, 'Get away from me,'
The nurse said, 'would you wait outside,
I'll call you when there is something to see.'

So I waited, and waited, as time went by,
'Oh! Why, does it take so long?'
The nurse came out and said to me, 'Be patient
The pains are now quite strong.'

Oh! My goodness, I couldn't take any more,
I wiped the sweat from my brow,
'Surely,' I said to myself,
'Something must be happening by now.'

Then all of a sudden, I heard a cry,
And the nurse came running out,
'You have a son,' she said to me,
'Hurry now, don't hang about.'

I walked into the labour ward and I saw,
My wife and our beautiful son,
She looked at me with love in her eyes,
And said, 'Look what I have done.'

I said I was sorry she had so much pain
Then she said, 'It was not so bad,'
She said she would do it all again for me,
She was so happy she had made me a Dad.
Stephanie Harvey

My Father the Bus Driver

My Father, the bus driver, would knot my school tie
And shoelaces at seven o'clock and kiss me goodbye and,
At eight, he'd pull up just down the road in his big green bus
I'd join the end of the queue and when my turn came
I'd climb aboard and give him a huge smile
Keeping my pass in my pocket
I'd let the others sit down and would proudly hold onto the rail
Past the sign which said, *No Passengers Beyond This Point*
I'd ignore the request not to speak to the driver
And as the seats emptied, still I would rather stand
As the school stop approached all the other children
Would appear in a huge cluster from upstairs
Still munching their early morning breakfast of crisps and sweets
But the bus didn't go to the normal stop
It pulled up right outside the school gates
The children spilled like beans onto the path
They would turn and say thank you
For the five extra minutes before class
And then it was my turn to get off
As I did some of the children would ask
'Do you know that man?'
And, brimming with pride, I'd say
'Yes, he's my Dad.'

Jenny Avery

To Dad

To dear Dad, one of a kind
In his garden you will find.
All kinds of plants and flowers
There he would spend many hours
When I was young and full of fun
Tales he would tell me in the sun
Wisdom and kindness, of this he is full
But at times he played the fool.
Sitting there by this man
Love of him you can understand
Working with his hands every day
Bright and cheerful, never grey
Wood he would take and put into shape
To see him in action, it was great
Chair and tables, all of wood
Stories he would tell when he could
Years go by and take their toil
As a Dad, he's great in this role
Now is the time for him to rest
He's one of, if not the best
Love and affection, his still to give
In his company, a thrill to live.
Dear Dad we love you more and more
More than ever than before.

C Threader

A Father's Wish

That you may have till you depart
A healthy mind, a healthy heart
A wealth of love that hèlps you do
The best for others worse than you

That you may have a steady wit
A helping hand for those unfit
A caring hand to help the poor
A praying hand for those at war

A spotless body, soul and mind
A thirst for knowledge and to find
A wealth of love in all you do
And faith to help you see it through

That you may have when'er you speak
A voice that champions for the weak
A selfless labour for your task
Of helping those too tired to ask

That you may savour all these things
And know that you can walk with kings
Then after all's been said and done
You'll know that you've been rich, my son.

Norman Whittle

We Loved Mondays

Every Monday to Friday you got on your bike,
a sheet-metal worker I think you worked hard
I scrubbed your overalls in the backyard.
You was a joking, laughing, really nice man,
from Monday to Friday things were just fine.
When pay day came around a few quid was slung
to you wife and four kids, thought your duty done.
The pub just a few doors away
eventually got all the rest of your pay.
Shaved, dressed up, you looked real fine,
but rolled home skint most of the time.
Sharing your money between horses and ale,
the beer you supped would have filled a large pail.
Then lying prostrate on the couch or the floor,
sometimes not able to crawl to the door.
Thinking all fathers behaved in this way
we kept well hidden, busy at play.
Hush little children don't make a sound,
Monday morning will soon come around.
We had to be patient our time to bide
You was a typical case of *Jekyll and Hyde*.

Jean Barr

Our Mentor!

F is for *Father, Forthright, and Fair,*
A man of his word - and Just!
A is for *Able, Adept, and Adore,*
And a man, *all* feel they can Trust!
T is for *Talented, Tried and True* -
Artistic with Wit and Flair -
H is for *Handsome, Heart and Honour,*
A combination which today, - is so Rare!
E is for *Ethics - and for Esteem* -
Respected, and Cherished by all;
R is for *Revered, Resolute, and Reliant,*
With solicitude - for his family, so small!

This *commendation*, of our dear Father,
Whose tenacity knew no bounds!
Law-abiding! An exemplory fellow -
Responsible, optimistic and sound!

We emulated - *shining example!*
He took the *helm,* when storms rocked the boat -
At all times - *cool, calm and collected,*
'Twas *his guidance* - which kept us afloat!

He was bereft - after Mum died so young -
Yet - never flinched from what he must do,
For three *lost* little children, all under ten,
Dear Dad - we owe *all* to you!

Gertrude Parsons

For Gangy

I can't remember my Father, he left when I was three,
So I turned to my Grandad, who took me on his knee.
He became a better Father than the one to whom I was born,
He gave me joy and laughter with every day's new dawn.
He gave my life new meaning, he was my greatest friend,
I was his special darling, round my finger he I could bend.
If ever I faced trouble, to him I would run and hide,
I knew that I was safe and loved whilst he was by my side.
Oh I remember my Grandad, he was the best pal I ever had,
My lovely, sweet old Grandad, who became my Dad.

Avril Houlton

Dear Dad

Dear Dad,
Sorry I won't see you
On Sunday, Fathers' Day.
I really am so sorry
That I live so far away.

I'd love to come and visit,
We could go out for a walk,
Enjoy each others company
Together, laugh and talk.

I remember all the lovely times
When I was just a lad
And you were big and strong and tall
And proud to be my Dad.

Now all the years have quickly gone
And to a man I've grown,
Travelled half around the world,
I have children of my own.

Sorry I won't see you Dad,
I live so far away
But I send you all my heartfelt love
For a Happy Fathers' Day.

Patricia Catling

An Irish Father

With the sharpness of Shaw
and the humour of Wilde,
the airy, fairy-story, man
I remember as a child.

As abstract as Joyce
and as frank as O'Connor,
the riddle and the fiddle man
I bestow this in your honour.

Maureen O'Rourke

The Artful Dodger

Come on Dad get out of bed
It's Fathers' Day today,
Mum is getting breakfast
While the kids go out to play,
I've arranged a busy day for you
To keep you on your toes,
There's painting and there's papering
Then there's the lawn to mow,
I'd better go and check on him
I think he's still asleep,
I crept into the bedroom
And had a little peep,
I found his bed was empty
And a note was lying there,
To say that he'd gone fishing
But he didn't tell us where,
Oh well! He does deserve a break
He works hard at his chores
And he's such a loving Dad to have
So who could ask for more

S E Hardcastle

Father to a Travelling Child

So you came to me that Spring morn
And said to me, 'I'll soon be airborne,
To that land of Oz so far away,
For a year I want to stay.'

You my child of travelling ways,
I remembered then your early days.
Of struggles to find yourself
And hard work, to find wealth.

I wrestled with my thoughts that day.
Not wanting you to go away
But knew the strength of your desires,
That within you burnt like forest fires

And so off you went to Heathrow
With me there to see you go.
Fearing you would see me cry
I had to insist it was a passing fly

Back I went home with vacant seat
As you went off towards the heat
Quantas bound, with a stop at Bangkok.
My thoughts - had that case got a lock?

No letters for weeks - me going mad
Had you by white slavers been had
But no, then letters came thick and fast
You are in Oz, with a joy that will last

I relived my youth with your tales.
Daughter mine give me more details,
On life in that most marvellous land.
But return - again, to hold my hand.

John Wellings

The Same Old Dad to Me

My dear Dad is an OAP,
Face lined and gnarled like an ancient tree.
He's not bald yet, but his hair's turned grey,
He'll be seventy eight on his next birthday.

His hands no longer work the way they once did,
He finds it hard to unscrew the jampot lid.
He feels the cold in his poor old feet,
And he has some difficulty, rising from his seat.

He once used to be an upright gent,
But his lithe physique has sadly bent.
His eyesight's not what it used to be,
But he's *still* the same old Dad to me!

Sue Wingett

My Childhood Friend

Dad, I know you're near me
For I see you in my dreams.
I try to reach out to touch you,
But you fail to hear my screams.

I remember when I was a child,
How you comforted me in your arms,
I recall how I'd drift to sleep in them,
Knowing I was safe from harm.

I remember our trips to the park
Where we'd run and race around,
And stay out till long after dark,
Time, for us, was no bound.

I look back on these happy times
And realise how much I loved you.
I found it hard to tell you then,
But I hope and pray that you knew.

Now, it is too late, too late
To express to you my love,
But I hope that you are watching me
From your Heaven up above.

I'd love to be with you again,
For *you* were my childhood friend.

Deborah Ward

Fathers Day

Dear Daddy, how I love you
You'll never really know
All the seeds of kindness that you have truly sown
Are embedded in my memory, the thoughts of you run deep,
Now you're no longer with me, all I do is weep.
And on this very special day,
Though you're not here with me
You'll always be the only man who really does know me.

I wish that I had told you,
What a special Dad you are,
The day you died and left me
Will always bear the scar
But if you can still hear me,
I would like to say, you truly were the best Dad
So happy Fathers Day.

C Bampton

Dad's Dented Car

I'll take them to their party now
A job that seemed so easy
Until I heard that dreadful crunch
A noise that wasn't teasing
I knocked upon my own front door
A smile was all you showed
Until I broke that awful news
Your car's got dents you know
You shot outside
To see the harm
I'd done unto your wing
Oh no I did not want to see
The anger it would bring
I shook and shook
And cried a lot
But all to no avail
Your anger never showed to me
Here lies a sad old tale
So thanks for taking it so well
You probably felt like screaming
I never will forget the love
And in my heart its meaning

T Hennessey

A Dad of Yesteryear

A hardworking Black Country lad was my Dad,
The love of his family was all that he had,
He never expected a life filled with leisure,
Just simple things gave him much pleasure,
A cool glass of beer, a cigarette to smoke,
A chat with his friends, sharing a joke,
He had a talent unique for making folks glad,
When he was around, you could never be sad.
Family gatherings at Christmas were sheer delight,
In the middle of the room he'd stand up and recite,
The night I fought Jack Johnson and *Solly from Petticoat Lane*
Without his old time monologues Christmas never seems the same.
I remember him best from my childhood days,
Walking with him, and my brother, through woodlanded ways,
Through Hayseech Coppice and Haden Hill Park
Where he taught us to identify the thrush and the lark,
We'd pick bluebells to bring home and put in a jar,
How long ago it seems, and oh, so far.
Life moved then at a slower pace,
The things we learned then, time can never erase,
With our mother he taught us right from wrong,
To respect the folk we walked among.
Round the fireside when winters were cold and long,
He'd regale us with stories of when he was young,
His school-days, and First World War days in the Royal Marines,
We could imagine it all, those bygone scenes,
Thrilled by his tales we would eagerly implore,
'Again Dad - please tell it again, once more.'
Though he's gone and can't hear me, I still have to say
'Thank you Dad - Happy Fathers' day.'

Nancy Sheldon

My Father my Friend

Cricket on the garden lawn fishing in the pond.
Those and many more things Dad forged our special bond.
I used to call you Daddy I was you little lad.
Ours was the best relationship anyone could have.
Your little lad was growing up and then you called me Son.
The happy times of forming my early days now done.
You answered all my questions and taught me fair play.
Always had time for me though you'd had a busy day.
You guided with a Father's love through my rebellious years.
Showed me how to be myself and calmed my many fears.
Now I am a young man I look back on what we had.
And know now and forever my best friend is my Dad.

Sybil G Smithson

Who Knows!

Dad, I don't believe you,
With all your stupid rules!
My friends don't have to be in then
They're not treated like they're fools!

Dad, don't you know that times have changed
Since you were seventeen?
I'm really not a child you know
There's not much I haven't seen.

Dad, I know the places to avoid
Where there's drugs or there's a fight.
It's you who would not be street wise
I know that I am right!

Dad, hello. I'm sorry that it's late.
What time? It's half past three.
Where am I, now you're not to fuss,
I'm ringing from casualty.

Dad, no, don't worry. No, I'm fine,
It's my friend who has been hurt.
At the taxi rank, there was a knife,
A small cut but a ruined shirt!

Dad, will you really, are you sure?
You'll come, is that alright?
Perhaps I wasn't so grown up
And you were a little right!

Maggie Doré

Gone Home

You led us through the forest in those magic, youthful days
when the world was just beginning, years ago.
You left us signs to follow in those great untrodden ways
which only nature's chosen get to know.

There were arrows, there were crosses, made from gathered stones and sticks,
there were grasses tied in knots to show the way.
A stone within a circle when you'd used up all your tricks
and the sun had gone to rest at close of day.

Gone home, it said, the game is done;
I've taught you all I can
of how to follow in the tracks
of many a better man.

You led us through the game of life, when boyhood days were flown,
and the magic took a more mature disguise.
You gave us signs to follow that were still but scarcely known
as you took us in the footsteps of the wise.

A point within a circle, from which we cannot err,
equidistant from its fellows; chosen few.
A point within a circle to which we may refer
to find again the magic that was you.

A point within a circle,
the last and final sign.
Gone home, it said.
Gone home.

Bill Shorto

On Being a Dad

Being a Dad's not half so bad
As I thought when I was a lad
It has its depressions, sometimes the pits
With all my daydreams around me in bits
But when the family is well and spirits are high
All of our projects nearly finished and dry
It feel it's been worth it, the heartache and strife
With the best one beside me as always, my wife!

P Love

That's my Dad

Karate black belt, keep-fit fanatic,
pumping iron up in the attic.
Rearranging carols into rude verse,
taking time to rehearse and rehearse.
Out with the boys in shell suit clad.
That's my *Dad*.

Always hard up, never no money,
sense of humour, witty and funny.
On nappy changing he'll never grouse,
for we have a new baby in our house.
And when I'm naughty he's never mad.
That's my *Dad*.

Feeding the ducks up at the lake,
always there whenever I wake.
Snuggling close within his embrace,
looking up to his kindly face.
Whenever I cry, seeing him sad.
That's my *Dad*.

Going shopping, pushing the trolley,
me inside, holding my dolly.
Riding pillion on Dad's push bike,
these are the things I really like.
Kissing mummy, making her glad.
That's my *Dad*.

That's our Dad: Holliane and Joshua

Jacqueline A Hall

King of Kings

Because,
it's those we love the most,
that make our lives worthwhile.

Such,
golden days of happiness,
you bring Dad with your smile.

The,
understanding love you give,
so freely knows no bounds.

For,
me, you're King of all the Kings,
despite size of the crowds.

I,
salute you, an accolade,
you're what a Dad should be.

Pure,
gentleness, combined with strength.
Dad, you're the world to me.

Pamela Pitts

A Father's Greatest Treasure

I watch you sleeping peacefully there
And hold you in my arms and think
What a joy you are to me
I touch your cheek as soft as silk
Your hair is like spun gold
I hold your little body close
And rock you to and fro
I sing you songs and lullabies
And say you are Daddy's little boy
I see you smile your face alight
As you find new things a joy
I watch you toddle and stop your fall
I want to keep you from all harm
I know you are God's special gift to me
You give me so much pleasure
Of all the things that a Father could have
You are the greatest treasure.

Christine Isaac

Fatherhood

Our first meeting was nocturnal and for that you turned up late,
the hospital said 'Hurry!' but your shower couldn't wait!

You drove there like a maniac, arrived in quite a flap
and soon an irate midwife dumped me crossly on your lap.

I fear I didn't look my best, all wrinkled in a towel,
but I, in turn, thought you quite strange, and showed it with a howl!

Each night I woke - you weren't aware, you always slept right through,
until you woke to three heads on the pillow not just two!

You put my clothes on back to front, but still you tried your best,
and when you changed my nappy, got the tapes stuck to my vest!

Mum's routine changed, your meals, all late, were served up cold or black,
whilst on dark stairs you found my ball and slid down on your back!

At two I help you wash the car, to use the hose I'd beg,
I waxed your screen and washed your tapes then sprayed your trouser leg!

Your briefcase seemed the perfect place to put my clown away,
emerging at a meeting with your client and boss next day!

I helped to fill your shopping bags with soap like Mummy buys,
you could have been arrested if you'd not had such sharp eyes!

One day you said you'd lost your job, you seemed so cross and sad,
I hunted for it everywhere to stop you feeling bad.

It seemed you'd caught *redundancy* - I tried to make you well,
you fought to hide the way you felt, but I could always tell.

I stroked your beard and made you tiny plastic cups of tea,
but secretly felt happy whilst you stayed at home with me.

But now you leave at dawn and don't come home 'till I'm in bed,
I miss you but it's so that you can buy me things, Mum said.

Yes, Fatherhood's a tricky job, but you don't do too bad,
in fact I'd say, without a doubt, I'm proud that you're my Dad!

Lesley J Freeman

In Memory

With love I remember the times that we had
With tears in my heart I remember you Dad
You were the moon and sun to me
You helped me discover what I wanted to be
Ever there to shelter me from the rain
Ever there to smooth away my pain
A friend to reach out to when I felt low
A friend to support me when I'd had a hard blow
You took me to places I would never have seen
You made me consider the places I'd been
I so enjoyed your songs when I was a tot
I appreciated your loving ways a lot
You were my cushion for years and years
You were always around to wipe away my tears
My knight amongst men - Protector Supreme
My tower of strength, you helped me fulfil my dream
If you were still alive and could be here today
If you could see what I've achieved, I wonder what you'd say
I only know I'm so grateful, for the way I've turned out
I owe much to you Daddy, of that I've no doubt
As with love I remember the times that we had
With tears in my heart I remember you Dad.

Cherry Somers-Dowell

Fragile

It was Summer, an idyllic day
The season my Father passed away
My garden full of life and bloom
Death came in an impersonal hospital room.

Nine years the hurt is still as deep
I see his face before I sleep
The tattoos climbing up his arm
Instilling past days with tranquil calm.

He always had time to listen to what I had to say
He understood me very well, he had a certain way,
He told me life was fragile respect its delicacy
I always have, I always will a gentle manner had he.

For no one knows what's round the bend,
I stand alone without my friend
With great sadness your name I mouth
Oh how I loved you Daddy Alf.

I loved this man from beginning to end,
A part of me will never mend
Your death in my life left a hole
You were one of the few to know my soul.

Emile Ewe

Remember . . .

It didn't mean so much to me,
But meant a lot to him.
To reminisce of days gone by,
Of how things might have been.
He talked about how he had lived
And how his life began,
Of how he lived life to the full,
Before the war had stained the land.
Of how he'd joined the army
And later left to find,
A girl who became my mother,
A woman good and kind.
And as his eyes began to close,
I envied peace of mind,
To end a long and happy life,
With dreams of better times.

Paul Sanders

Daddy's Favourite Chair

So very many years ago
When I was only young,
I remember things that happened,
And songs my Father sung.

My Dad sat in his big armchair,
And I sat on his knee;
He sang the songs that were the rage
In days that used to be.

He sang to me old nursery rhymes,
The ones all children knew.
I asked to hear them all the time,
As children always do.

He told me lots of stories,
Sitting in that old chair -
I loved to listen to those tales
When I sat with him there.

I can't forget that old armchair,
It was my favourite time,
When Daddy held me on his knee,
And sang those songs sublime.

So when anybody asks me
About those times so fair,
I tell them that I can't forget
My Daddy's favourite chair.

Milly Blane

Dad

The years go by so quickly,
Don't think I've ever said,
The way I feel about you
The thoughts inside my head.

We shouldn't hide emotions,
Be they happy or blue,
I should put my arms around you, Dad,
And say that I love you.

It really should be simple,
To show we love and care,
Words aren't always easy,
Though we know they're always there.

I couldn't say I love you,
And now I wish I had,
I only hope you understood,
'Cause you've gone forever. . . Dad.

Maureen Biseker

To Daddy

Although I am an adult now,
And many years have past,
The love I hold for Daddy,
Is a love I know shall last.
For never mind how old I am,
I know one thing for sure,
I'll always need my Daddy near,
To make me feel secure.
It's true that every girl in life,
Will love another man,
But no one could mean more to me,
Than Daddy ever can.
The new friends that I have now met,
Have forced me to adjust,
But Daddy is the only man,
A girl can really trust.
A Daddy will not let you down,
Oh no, he's there for life,
To comfort and to hold you,
In times of pain and strife.
The feeling that I hold inside,
So strong that words can't show,
The father figure that I see,
Is one I do love so.
So Daddy please remember,
I love you from my heart,
You'll always be my special one,
Together or apart.

Kate Luckes

Letters to Dad

A, B, C.
D for Dad who comforts me.
E, F, G.
H for the happiness you gave so free.
I, J, K.
L for the love that was always mine.
M, N, O.
P for promises of better times.
Q, R, S.
T for troubles that spoilt our day.
U, V.
W for worry when you went away.
X.
Y for the yearning you'd come back to me one day.
Z, the end, no more to say.

Emma Shaw

Our Dad

We loved to sit and listen
To the stories he used to tell,
About when he was a little boy,
We remember them all so well.

His school-days were very haphazard
It cost a penny to go each day,
If his Mother was short of money,
(which often she was)
At home he had to stay.

But nevertheless he left school at ten,
On the farm with his Father he went,
He learned how to plough and milk the cows,
And to go where he was sent.

Then one day he met a land girl,
During the first world war,
That was how he became our Dad,
There was happiness evermore.

He called our mother *my lovely*
A name we can still hear him say,
He was such a kind and loving soul,
His example stays with us today.

He loved his family and his home,
He loved his garden too,
Although you're now not with us,
Dear Dad, we still love you.

Marie Daly

My Father

He sat in concentrating mood,
His briar pipe between his teeth,
His furrowed brow
Reflects the scene
Over the surrounding heath.
A gentle soul, his face now lined
Yet still defying the passing of time,
He ponders there upon the hill
His work now done, within the mill.

His blue eyes bright, surveyed them tall,
The blackened chimney's below
For all to see,
The smoke ascending there
In spirals grey, into the air.

What were your thoughts my Father dear?
As you sat, when you were here.
You left a memory divine,
Your soul still bright, entwined in mine.
I recall so well your jolly laugh,
Your coming down our homeward path,
A bag of sweets within your grasp,
A treat for us, as night-time passed.

Your face still shines within my mind,
As a stalwart beacon of mankind,
A prop to follow, that is just,
Until I too . . . become
As dust.

Jenny Horrocks

Dear Dad

I'll start by saying thank you Dad
For always being there,
For sharing all my problems
You've always showed you care.

Ever since I was a child
Whether I was good or bad,
You've always been there for me
And for that I'm really glad.

You've made me laugh when I've cried
Through arguments and fear,
I know I can depend on you
To me you are so dear.

So thank you once again dear Dad
For teaching me all I know,
You've always been a good Dad
And for this I love you so.

Katie French

My Dad

He's like a giant he stands so tall,
This man so big and me so small,
He jags my cheek with his sandpaper face,
And he locks me tightly in a strong embrace,
He swings me about like an old rag doll,
Yet he never hurts me, not at all,
He tells me he loves me this man I adore,
With a heart like a lion but gentle to the core,
He is my hero, I'm his little lad,
This idol of mine is my Dad.

E Larkin

If Only?

Being a Dad is a difficult task,
I never quite know what you're going to ask,
And try as I might to live up to your dreams
Of what a Dad should be, it just never seems
As if I can fulfil your expectations,
I am aware of my own limitations.

I could do nothing to further your cause -
Perhaps I was going through the Male Menopause -
When you wanted a partner for billiards or pool,
A game of badminton, or help at school,
I was always too busy to spare you the time,
I can never recapture what could have been mine.
If only I'd stopped and counted the cost -
Too late I realised what I had lost.

If only? Too late! How often I've heard,
The remorse imbued in these saddest of words!
But Tempest Fugit, you've all flown the nest,
We look to the future and hope for the best,
All my misgivings belong to the past -
Now I'm a Grandfather - I'm a *Grand Dad*, at last!

Nancy Gray

Seaside Memories

I grabbed the rolled up trouser leg,
He bent and swung me o'er his head,
And raced beside the ebbing tide,
With me astride his back so wide,
I sang just like a bird in flight,
He laughed and held me very tight,
I shouted out, he grabbed my hand,
Then puffed and panted, ran and ran.
He was the steed and we would fly,
Up to the Heavenly, bright, blue sky.
But then he stumbled, stopped and coughed,
He pulled me down from up aloft,
'See here, young miss, you're only four,
Your Dad is thirty years and more,
So take my hand and let us walk
Along the shore, and we can talk,
And when you're grown and see the sea,
Remember piggy back and me.'

Isobel MacCallum

Fathers Day Roses

In 1910 Mrs Bruce Dodd,
thought of offering thanks to God,
for all the Fathers of her land
so she had a special service planned.
On that great day, each girl and boy,
wore a rose to show their joy.
In 1916, America's President
had bouquets of roses sent,
to Fathers far away from home,
from the lands finest gardens grown.
The rose became a symbol of the day
as America lead the way
for other Nations to join in,
with their Fathers' Day offerings.
Now it's a joy that we all share,
showing our Fathers that we care.
What if the gifts be large or small,
when there is love behind them all.

Pat Rissen

So Many Loving Hearts

I stood at the railway station holding my Mother's hand,
On the platform that dull, foggy day, was a small brass band,
They were coming home they told us, home from fighting a war,
Can somebody please explain, fighting a war, what for?

I'd never known my Daddy for I was born while he was away,
And now at four years old he was coming home to stay,
My Mother was excited, I could not understand why,
I felt so alone and insecure I just wanted to cry.

The train came into the station and doors were flung open wide,
Here was the young husband coming home to his lovely bride,
Here was a little girl, so afraid and so alone,
Here was a stranger standing there, someone I'd never known.

He picked me up and cuddled me and told me he was glad,
For to be home at last, he could start to be, a proper kind of Dad,
I backed away and tried to hide behind my Mother's skirt,
The toy panda he had brought home for me, fell into the dirt.

I wondered how he must have felt travelling all that way,
Coming home at last to his lovely wife and little girl that day,
The disappointment of his little girl so distant and afraid,
Oh, what a difference a big hug and a lovely smile would have made.

We never really made up for all those years we lost,
For one thing is for certain, war has its human cost,
The rejection of his daughter was far more than he could bear,
But she was only little then, was his judgement fair?

We've put it all behind us now and try to show we care,
But really the damage has been done, it is a sad affair,
War affects the lives of everyone, everyone takes a part,
It kills, maims, destroys and breaks so many loving hearts.
Jacqui Weeks

The Hero

When sons become Fathers
As mine have done,
Every day is *Fathers' Day*
To their little ones.
Daddy is his greeting,
As he returns from work,
Tired and weary,
Not being one to shirk
Duties however arduous,
Varied or mundane,
Carry on regardless,
Even if in pain.
Father is a hero
To his young son,
Footballing, cycling,
All the games are fun,
Planning the holidays,
Mowing the lawn,
Every day is *Fathers' Day*
From the day the child is born.

Frances Hickman-Robinson

Remembering a Special Dad

When you spoke we all stood to attention
But your actions spoke louder than words
A tall upstanding person
Well seen, and always heard
But you had a heart of gold
Everyone could see
You deserved the very best in life
But alas that could not be
Why did you have to leave us
You had so much to give
You are with us wherever we go
Your memory will always live
With all of us to treasure
Loving thoughts of you
So true
You left a space
No man could fill
There was only one
Like you.

Rose Froud

Fathers Day

You wouldn't want red roses or to go out for a meal,
But we thought we'd try to tell you something of how we feel
We'd like to thank you Daddy for all your loving care,
No one else could take your place, thanks for just being there,
When we have a problem we always come to you,
And with your special magic you know just what to do,
You try to keep us happy when we know sometimes you're sad,
We're not always angels - sometimes we drive you mad,
We're young and headstrong and at times think we know it all,
But your loving arms enfold us and catch us when we fall,
We know it's not been easy - sometimes it's been a struggle
To come to terms and sort things out when life is just a muddle.
The skies will not always be grey and when our ship comes in,
We'll laugh and talk about the times we faced life with a grin,
We'll do our best to follow a path that's straight and true,
And when we grow up Daddy - we want to be like you.

Ruby A Houghton

Our Dad

He isn't much to look at.
He stammers when he talks.
His clothes are quite old-fashioned.
And he wobbles when he walks.
He used to be a *dandy*.
When we were in our teens.
Until the slump of the 30's.
When we sank, to lower *means*.
We know, he always loves us.
Puts on a brave new face.
In spite of all his problems.
That burdened his lifes' pace.
And now that he is aging.
Is looking, somehow, *small*.
Those are the days we love the best.
When *Our Dad* comes to call.

Joy Philips

To my Father . . .

Today somebody asked me what my Father means to me
I never quite considered it before.
I take for granted that you head my family
And now I think about it you're much more.
I can't envisage life without your presence
That safe warm feeling knowing you are near
My confidence when I have got a grievience
My comforter when I am close to tears.
You entertain me with your funny stories
I've loved you for as long as I recall.
I know without a doubt you love me
I'm proud of you and now I love you more.
I guess I love you not 'cause you're my Father
But because there is a bond of love and care.
And I know that there is nobody I'd rather
Watch over me my hopes and dreams to share . . .

Sonia Santina

A Father's Love

A Father is your comfort when you're small
His fortitude becomes your safety net;
He will always ignore your little downfalls
And never view your failures with regret.

He will be the first to share your happiness;
He's a man that will know your every mood,
Yet when you pour your heart out to him
He will neither condemn you nor intrude.

He will calm you in your very darkest hours
And carry you through your times of pain,
Yet when rebuffed with indignations of your youth,
When you need him, he will come right back again.

From a distance he will see your life take shape
And watch you as you're coming into bloom;
And when a man asks to take you for his wife
He will always say he's come along too soon!

He will sit for hours on end with good advice,
When you go to him for endless admonition
And at the end when you walk the other way
His blessing he'll still give with absolution.

There'll be many times when words are left unspoken
But there's always something special that you share,
And even when the miles have come between you;
If you look over your shoulder he'll be there.

Caren Jayne

Don't Judge Me - Just Love Me

Please my Son don't judge me
For the innocence of my youth
Please don't ever blame me
Because our time has stole the truth

For you I did my best my Son
Although at times I got it wrong
Our lives were not made easy
But it's to me that you belong

When you came I was not ready
But what love I had we shared
The cards were stacked against us
I was young, unlived and scared

Please try to understand me
And don't be quick to turn my knife
Because on the day your Mum gave birth to you
Was the first day of my life.

Donna Masterton

The Important Man

Treasure your Father while you may,
For some day he may have to go away,
Not from choice, but by God's plan,
Then you will miss that important man.

He cherished you when you were small,
And encouraged you into walking tall,
He taught what's right and what is wrong,
For sight of him you might sometimes long.

From him wise lessons you have learned,
For his comforting arms you sometimes yearned,
So enjoy and love him while you can,
And value that most important man.

Glenda Lawrence

Daddy, Daddy

Daddy can I have it
Please Dad can I have it
Dad I really need it
You wouldn't be cruel, would you?

Daddy I'd like to do it
I would Dad, wouldn't you
Daddy I've got to do it
You will come Dad, won't you?

Daddy I didn't do it
I didn't do that at all
Daddy I couldn't have done it
I'm much too, much too small

M P Newman

Our Daddy

We love our Daddy, he is so tall
Makes our Mummy look very small.

He mends our bikes, and all our toys
And never complains when we make a noise.

It's Dad do this and Dad do that,
No wonder he never has time to chat.

He works all day and sometimes nights,
But always finds time to help fly our kites.

He joins us in football, and cricket too,
And sometimes on Saturdays we go to the Zoo.

He washes the car, and mows the lawn,
And there's piles of wood that has to be sawn.

Then he climbs the ladder and washes the panes,
That are all dirty with wind and rain.

He is ever so busy this Dad of ours,
Who works so hard for hours and hours.

If we didn't have him what would we do,
Poor Mummy would cry, and I think we would too.

Hazel Lancaster

Fathers Day

My son went to the shops one day
And bought a card for Fathers' Day.
When he got home, he sat and wrote
Inside the card, this little note:
Dear Dad, I just want to say
I'm thinking of you every day.
Not just on one day in the year
When summertime will soon be here.
I think about the rugby games,
The bonfire that went up in flames,
The happy days upon the beach,
And cricket balls hit out of reach,
Toasting crumpets by the fire,
Losing oars when boats we'd hire.
I love you, Dad, and always will
And wish that you were with us still.
But now you live with God above
And He will give you all my love.

My Son was only twelve that day
When he bought a card for Fathers' Day.

Frances Russell

A Father
(A dedication to my Daughters)

What more could a Father need
To make his life complete
Than two wonderful daughters
Who are so beautiful and sweet,

What more could a Father ask
What could be more dear
Than the love of his daughters
A love innocent and sincere,

What more could a Father dream
Than to see his daughters grow
From childhood into young ladies
Knowing that they love him so,

What more could a Father find
What fortune could be worth
More than the richness of his children
Which he found at their birth,

What more could a Father be
Than a comfort and a friend
And a shelter to his children
Right to the very end,

What more could a Father want
What more could he ever need
Than to see his children blossom
The living results of his seed.

D Best

Memories on Fathers Day

I miss you, Father, on this day;
You were my hero, in every way,
And precious memories, of you, I recall,
Back in my childhood - I treasure them all.

I remember the doll - it was after the War,
(Wrapped in a shawl), that I used to adore;
You must've spent hours, to make it look good,
Just to please me - you had carved it in wood!

One night on your knee, I'll never forget;
The times were hard, and we were in debt;
No longer the farm, you thought we could hold,
But my pony, you said, would never be sold!

I was your favourite, of this I could tell,
For you couldn't disguise it very well;
With you in my corner, I really felt proud,
But I never expressed my feelings aloud.

You taught me to drive, both tractor and car,
You gave me the wheel, when we went afar;
And happy I was - in the harvest field,
Helping you then, to bring in the yield.

You cheered me up - never left me alone
When I was injured and far from home;
I wanted to say, but the words never came -
Just that I loved you, all over again.

A wonderful Father, and a friend of mine:
I'll never forget our home at the Bine:
I broke my heart, but you made me believe -
After you'd gone - I was not to grieve.
Irene Telfer

The Joy's of Being a Dad

It's great being a Dad,
just being the one who cares,
and was it you, who left those skates,
halfway down the stairs.

The pets you bring home are wonderful,
and we really loved that cat,
so don't take this the wrong way love,
you can't keep the big white rat.

The look of sheer delight,
that spread across your face,
when you pulled that bit of cotton,
and off fell all the lace.

You look real good, in those old clothes,
and your mothers new high heels,
and both your feet walked different ways,
I wonder how that feels.

And what about those worms,
did they really taste that good,
but worst of all the telling off,
for playing in the mud.

So now we come to bed time,
you're fast asleep and snoring,
before you were born I'm very sure,
that life was really boring.

Walter McGoff

A Man of Brass

Our Father was a man of brass,
I say *was*, because he's dead.
My Ma could have married a gentleman,
But she chose our Dad instead.
He worked as hard as any man,
He worked till he was old.
Our Father was a man of brass,
But he had a heart of gold.

Our Father was a man of brass,
He kept us clothed and fed,
He'd wash the brass dust from his hands
And shake it from his head.
His shirt was yellowed from the dust,
His boots were dusty too.
Dad, you did a lot for us,
What did we do for you?

Our Father was a man of brass,
At thirty six he died.
He left our Mother with nothing
But her stubbornness and pride,
She'd tell us proudly that when God
Made Dad, they broke the mould;
She'd say, 'Yer dad was a man of brass,
But he had a heart of gold.'

Robert Houghton

Patient Love

Run to the end of the road,
Wait expectantly;
Here he comes,
Jump excitedly;
He puts me on his bike,
He holds me tight and wheels me home.

Clamber into his special chair,
Wait eagerly;
Comb his hair, put in ribbons,
He sits patiently
Then takes me on his knee,
He holds me close and cuddles me.

Broken doll to be repaired,
Watch anxiously;
Willing hands work to mend
Skillfully.

Bedtime comes,
He lifts me in his arms,
He holds me near and kisses me;
Sleep peacefully.

Early memories of Dad.

Cynthia Dickens

Daddy's Here

I'm lying in bed, I'm aged about four
I'm scared, there's a witch standing close to the door.
I hide 'neath the sheets and I tremble with fear,
Two arms hold me close,
Daddy's here.

I'm coming from school, some bullies give chase,
They're older than I, for them it's no race.
Can't think what to do, my brain has gone numb,
A hand touches mine,
Daddy's come.

I'm doing exams, my head's in a whirl,
I'm an absolute duffer, the stupidest girl,
Am I really that bad or is it just nerves?
Relax, you're OK,
Daddy observes.

I look in the mirror, I'm dressed all in white,
Will I make a good wife, am I doing what's right?
It's pre-wedding nerves, stop these silly games,
You'll be wonderful, dearest,
Daddy exclaims

As I hold my new babe and we look at each other,
I pray I will be a success as a Mother,
It's fine at the moment and all very thrilling,
But will I need help?
Dad's willing

Please let me go daughter. There's no need to cry,
You must help me now. Be brave; say goodbye.
Think of me sometimes and when you do, dear,
I promise, my own girl,
Dad will be near.

Margaret Myttion

Father Figure

Bread-winner out at the crack of dawn
returning late, tired and forlorn.
What does he know of the games they played,
places they've been to, friends who stayed?
All day he has toiled to give them this life,
with joy in abundance and minimal strife.

He enters their room to whisper *goodnight*,
they jump up in bed, turn on the light
and beg him to read a favourite story,
exciting, delighting, a little big scary!
These moments are precious, the children and he
indulge in the comfort of shared fantasy.

Weekends are different, they'll walk in the park
and race to the swings, just for a lark.
He'll eat his fish fingers and *pick up* his peas,
play in the garden - end up on his knees!
Doing the things he missed with his Dad,
enjoying the freedom he never had.

Jennifer Allen

Hugs and Kisses

You were my Dad, I was your daughter
I wanted to be your friend
You kept your distance - no kisses, no cuddles
Oh Dad you would never bend.

In my heart I always cried out for
The Father I loved just to say
That he loved me too so very much
But you held your feelings at bay.

You were a good Dad, as Fathers go
You clothed and fed me, you were always there
I was never beaten, I never went cold
I could find no fault with your care.

Dad, I just needed a hug, the occasional kiss
I needed the warmth of your touch
But I was too shy, I couldn't reach out
I feel we missed out on so much.

Then I grew up, got married, had kids
I kissed and hugged them each day
All the love I'd held back over the years
I let go of and gave it away.

You then became ill and my heart it cried out
For still you would not let me touch you
You were stubborn and brave right to the end
And my love and respect for you grew.

I was there at your bed the night that you died
It broke my heart, you were fading so fast
But when your laboured breath expired
I got to hold you and kiss you at last.
Jan Stearn